To my gorgeous Nicola! love Lutz x

spend less, sell more

YOUR ONE-PAGE PLAN TO CONVERT MORE LEADS INTO SALES

Nicola Lutz

Reviews

"Sales is everyone's business and everyone can learn something from this book, not least how to manage your clients professionally from the initial contact to a deeper working partnership. For those new to sales it is a brilliant starting point and for those who are long in the tooth and think they know it all already, it is a fantastic reminder that, actually, there is always more we can do better! I wish I had had this book to hand when I started out, I will certainly be gifting it to all those in my team involved in sales!"

Lisa James, Managing Director, EC Young Learners, International

"This book really made me think about my sales process like a pro, and made me a million times better at following up and closing sales.Nicola lives and breathes sales strategy and walks her talk every day. This is tried and tested in the real world stuff, and it works."

Helen Tudor, LinkedIn Strategist

"This book feels more like a personal coaching session than a 'self-help' guide. Throughout this wonderfully informative and practically helpful book, I felt that Nicola was there with me. Coaching and coaxing me all the way to success. What I also got was strong sense of her conviction. Nicola knows that she can help me and just can't wait to get started. This all led to a joyfully optimistic and inspiring journey of self-reflection; facilitating the sharing of hard-won experience and providing a flawless plan which drives simply remarkable results.This is the one business book that you simply can't afford not to read."

Peter Hayes, MD of IH Manchester, UK

"Nicola cuts through the noise, highlighting the obvious but over looked difference between lead generation and the sales process. This book brings into sharp focus the important process of setting out your framework to initially qualify, and then diligently follow up with your leads to ensure this valuable resource becomes an asset and isn't left to waste in the land of the "Mind Monkeys."

Danny Silvester, CEO, Inline International

"Reading Nicola's book is like a breath of fresh air. It's written in a way that really stuck with me. It answers questions I didn't know I had, it changed my perception of rejection, 'no' is not bad. I no longer think I need to rush follow ups so I can get more leads in, but rather work smarter with the ones I have.A beautifully written book, in the very unique style Nicola has. It felt like she was sitting next to me, talking me through it. I cannot recommend this book enough, it's packed with value, fun to read and a book I'll definitely go back to regularly. A must for any sales person out there."

Lesinda Leightley, Director English test Marketing at PSI Services, International

"Nicola has succeeded with this book in erecting a mirror in which any individual immersed in the field of sales will contemplate themselves, deconstructing the 'salesperson,' their fears, uncertainties, and traumas that reside in the deepest corners of our being, subjecting them to analysis, and providing tools to skilfully address the vulnerable aspects of our sales strategy and approach. This book becomes essential reading for those venturing into the world of sales, as well as for those wishing to review and refine their skills, aspiring to attain mastery in the 'art of persistence.' Bravo, Nicola, you have created a masterpiece."

Ramon Villa, Language Kingdom, Spain

"Nicola Lutz has undoubtedly written THE sales book for the study travel industry! Nicola's genuine understanding of the lives, loves, and frustrations of every kind of seller and buyer in this sector make this book extraordinary.

The book is packed with Nicola's decades of sales and sales training experience and filled with all the very best sales practices. If you're in sales (no matter what you call it!), you need to read this book and do what Nicola says. Every single thing she says!Your boss will thank you,your bank account will thank you and, most importantly,your clients will thank you.

It's super readable and it's super doable! Every chapter is packed with the very best sales guidance that is made so clear and not a word of it is corny, overhyped, or sleazy sales. It's a down to earth and fun read that will not only help you sell far more and far more easily, you'll understand what your clients want and need from a sales process so much better.

It's a complete sales framework and Nicola has made it so simple and easy to follow. She's cut through the jargon, cut out all the corniness and sleaze, and cut to the chase with the sales gold! There are so many invaluable examples and real-life scenarios for each technique, that it's foolproof.

Spend Less, Sell More *is going to be required reading for any sales person who works with me!"*

Ian Aird, CEO, Universal English College, Australia

"Sales is sometimes seen as somehow incompatible with education. As if we can just keep the moral high ground and in some way our classrooms will fill themselves. This book shows that you can build it, but they won't come. Not unless you employ the systematic, logical and wholly ethical practices outlined in these pages. I recommend it for everyone, but especially for SME's who "don't get around" to sales. Buy this book, and you will."

Kevin McNally, President of IALC, Managing Director of IH Torquay, UK

"This book should be part of your team's training - a fantastic and inspiring pocket bible that makes you want to get up and sell like you have never sold before. Nicola's insights into the industry and sales in general are both thought provoking and inspiring. A recommended read for anyone linked to sales. "

Adelle Barnett, Learn Away Tours, UK

"This book does not only help new professionals to understand sales in education but reminds established salespeople of what is important. It is all about relationship building and human interaction in a digital world that makes processes easier but also allows us to forget what is essential to close a sale. Great book to read!"

Johanna Ziegler, Director of Admissions, Merrick Preparatory School, Canada

"This book feels being sat down and chatting to your best mate. It's direct, it's easy to follow and GETS YOU. Whether it's wrestling with 'mindset monkeys' or sweeping away the things that hold us all back. There's succinct, easy to implement wisdom here, and I'm glad I read it. But it's delivered with warmth, she knows what's it's like and that some bits work for different people "I'll do me, you do you" is a phrase I've now borrowed often!).This is crystal clear, tickets to success, from the guru to gurus."

Thom Jones, Director, Brock Solutions Agency

"Nicola's done a great job of getting the right tone - her personality and the jokiness she would add in person shines through; mixed with the science, data and practical aides to make you more effective. I do remember one of the hardest things was the resilience, not taking it personally but persevering - I wish I'd had these tools in my box of tricks and her voice in my head to help me keep going with the follow-up.

I also appreciated the examples - it made it more identifiable; and relatable from our industry."

Emma Hoyle, Managing Director, International House World Organisation, International.

"Nicola has been my friend for years. But, this is NOT singing her false praises. She gives a formidable, step by step, hands-on knowledge of how to take one out of one's comfort zone and place one firmly on the road to making more sales.

I have participated in her post-Covid sales challenges and it was a great help of taking me out of the doom and gloom state of mind and back to reality – I have a great product and people ARE interested.

Her book is a veritable fountain of sales tips and processes we all need to refer to from time to time just as reminder on how to stay on the road to success. AND it is a great read!"

Magdalena Jugovic, Executive Director, KUB Travel, Europe

"If you are a business owner and you want to make money, read this book.

No seriously, this book will make you realise just how much money you are leaving on the table and how easy it is to tap into once you nail your follow-up.

Honestly, this gem of a book will unveil the almost unlimited opportunities you've been unknowingly overlooking and show you how effortless it can be to grasp them once you master your follow-up skills.Personally, I considered myself quite adept at following up with potential clients; however, Nicola sheds light on the entire process, addressing even the peskiest of mental barriers, all while keeping it witty, engaging, and completely devoid of unnecessary fluff.She tackles every doubt, hurdle, and internal contradiction head-on, compelling you to sift through your CRM for leads you can't wait to pursue.

Paul Green, Founder, Client Funnels

ISBN: 978-1-7384685-0-8 (Paperback)
ISBN: 978-1-7384685-1-5 (Kindle)

Published 2023

Edited by Hugh Barker

Cover and interior design by Andy Meaden meadencreative.com

Contents

Introduction

I understand. Time is precious, and sales may not come naturally to you. Or maybe you've been selling for ages and are just curious to see if you can improve. Fear not! *Spend Less, Sell More* is intended to be your secret weapon, empowering you to stop chasing shiny marketing strategies and maximise the potential of your existing leads. By the time you reach the final page, you'll have your very own personalised Framework to optimise your sales process, increase revenue, and achieve sustainable growth – all within the constraints of your busy schedule.

There is simply no need for sleazy tactics or complex systems. My goal is simple: to help you leverage those valuable leads you've already paid for in all your social media marketing, events, and genius campaigns. You need to nurture relationships further and guide them towards closing the deal. Packed with actionable strategies and practical advice, this book is your key to re-engaging those quiet leads that you would otherwise have given up on and transforming them into loyal customers.

You might be thinking, "I don't have time to learn about sales!" or "Seriously, I've been selling for years," and I get it. That's why "*Spend Less, Sell More*" is designed for busy entrepreneurs and small businesses like yours. I won't overwhelm you with complicated tools.

Whether you have a CRM or just a trusty spreadsheet, along with your preferred social media channels, a phone, email, and a reliable calendar, I'll show you how to make the most of what you already have. It's all about practicality and getting results.

Consider this book your ultimate follow-up playbook, packed with real-life case studies and proven techniques. No fluff, just straightforward insights that will help you spend less time, money, and effort while boosting your sales conversion rates. Together, we'll develop a one-page Follow-Up Framework that keeps your leads engaged and propels them toward becoming paying customers.

While reading the book, you will probably realise that you have left a plethora of leads on the table that could have been converted. And I understand that reaching out after a long silence can feel as awkward as discovering spinach in your teeth AFTER a meeting. But fear not! I'll be your trusty sidekick, guiding you every step of the way with a playful yet professional approach.

You'll find real-life examples and case studies sprinkled throughout, illustrating how these strategies have transformed businesses just like yours. I'll prove that even the most dormant leads can be resurrected, turning them into raving fans who not only become paying customers but also refer their friends to you!

So, grab a cuppa and get ready for the journey. With "Spend Less, Sell More" as your trusty guide, you'll navigate the follow-up universe like a skilled adventurer, armed with humour, confidence, and, most importantly, an action plan for success. Together, we'll banish awkwardness, conquer silence, and reignite the spark within your leads.

Why read this book, and why bother crafting a one-page Follow-Up Framework?

- **You want to get 80% of possible sales, not 10%**
  Bring it on.
- **You want more sales and lower costs.**
  Do you want 50% more sales-ready leads at 33% lower cost?Yes please.
- **You want to be the go-to choice when leads are ready to buy.**
  So it's time for patient, persistent nurturing.
- **You want leads to make bigger purchases.**
  That'd be nice, right?

Okay then – are you with me? Ready to roll your sleeves up and get to work? Fantastic!

PART I: Conquer Mindset Challenges

In the world of sales, where charisma meets strategy and persuasion intertwines with persistence, it's easy to believe that every successful salesperson possesses an unshakable, unwavering mindset. Simply born with the sales swagger they can be seen at every event 'working the room' with a facade of confidence and resilience - which often obscures the very real challenges that lurk beneath the surface. It's a world where the show must go on, and vulnerability is rarely invited to the stage. Which is a shame.

We feel the relentless pressure to meet targets and quotas, even in the trickiest of times. The fear of rejection, the creeping self-doubt that sometimes whispers, "Am I good enough?" or "Is my service good enough?". The always present niggle that the competition might have got to that prospect first, upped their game or be discounting more heavily. There is an internal tug-of-war between being persistent and being perceived as pushy. We are expected to be gurus in our field, and yet often we landed in a sales role without any training or foundation, no formal knowledge of how sales works as a function and the (more boring?) parts of the role, and to admit it would be embarrassing, show a weakness, and that would never do.

These are the mindset challenges that many salespeople face, yet they are frequently shrouded in silence. Why? Because in the sales world, acknowledging these struggles can feel like exposing weakness, like admitting that you might not have it all together. It's a world where maintaining the facade of invincibility often takes precedence over personal growth and well-being.

But herein lies the paradox: it is precisely in embracing and addressing these challenges that true strength is found. In acknowledging vulnerability or gaps in your training, you open the door to resilience. In confronting self-doubt, you pave the way for unwavering confidence.

So, as we embark on this journey through the landscape of sales mindset challenges, remember this: you are not alone in these struggles, and there's no shame in facing them. In fact, it's a crucial step towards becoming a sales champion. Nobody else needs to know if you don't want to discuss it – it can remain in the pages of this book. Let's lift the veil a little, embrace the challenges, and harness the power of an empowered, resilient, and thriving sales mindset.

Chapter 1
Embracing the "No"

"Success is 90% failure."

– Soichiro Honda

Unless you convert every single lead you ever find, and you manage to onboard every cold outreach you've ever made, you are going to come across the answer "no".

"No" is part of sales. It's part of any business, whether you are actively selling or not – there is a natural churn in your client base, and this is completely normal.

Don't get me wrong, I can still get a little pouty if I've been utterly convinced someone was going to say 'yes' after we've done all due discovery and match making. And then they've said no. I mean… it seems so unfair (whines like a teenager...). But it passes faster now!

So then, we're going to tackle the inevitable "no" with our heads held high and our spirits soaring. Get ready to brush off those negatives, laugh like a James Bond baddie in the face of adversity, and turn every "no" into a stepping stone toward a resounding "yes."

It's Not Personal, Just a No for Now

When you hear that dreaded word, "no," don't let it shatter your confidence. Repeat after me: "It's not personal; it's just a no for now." Usually, they don't even know you. And even if they do know you, they have to also know, like and trust your team to deliver the service or product. Unless you've been rude and obnoxious, it's rarely going to be a "no" because of you. Have some faith in yourself!

Sometimes, the stars aren't aligned, and the customer might not be ready for your awesomeness just yet. And you need to know that 50% of buyers are a great fit for you, but simply aren't ready to buy yet. YET. (I've put it in shouty capitals, so you remember it!) So, take a deep breath, keep that smile on your face, and move on like the sales rockstar you are!

Learning from the "No "

As the great Thomas Edison once said, "I have not failed. I've just found 10,000 ways that won't work." Every "no" is simply a stepping stone on the path to success. It's all part of the journey. So, keep pushing forward, learn from each experience, and remember that, with every "no," you're getting closer to that resounding "YES!" Embrace the challenges, conquer the obstacles, and trust in the process; soon, you'll find yourself celebrating those well-earned victories.

Now, what I like to do is keep a record of objections, of why they have said no. They won't always tell you – but maybe they will. Often, they will cite "budget", but this can be a smokescreen, or an easy way out. I suspect they usually haven't quite understood the value. If you can dig around a little more to uncover their true objection this will help. These objections and obstacles are likely to come up time after time, so once a week, workshop them – find ways to eliminate them before they are even mentioned by your lead. Or, maybe there is something in your offer that they aren't understanding quickly enough. Or they're not seeing the value in the outcome they'll benefit from. Or perhaps it is you after all (sorry!), and your offer or product needs to be tweaked or redeveloped?

Detach yourself emotionally from the outcomes of your outreach – use each rejection as a learning opportunity. And, in fact, a marketing opportunity – no outreach is ever entirely wasted.

Maintaining the Relationship after a "No"

So, you got a "no". Big deal. It's not the end of the world; it's the beginning of a beautiful friendship. If they were a qualified lead, they were a good fit for your offer. After the rejection, reach out and show some love with a heartfelt thank you. Keep the communication channels open, keep adding value, and keep in touch. That "no" might turn into an "I'm ready for ya" down the road. Keep it friendly, stay genuine, and watch those connections blossom.

Celebrating the "No"

Time to switch that mindset again. Firstly, each "no" is a milestone, a sign that you're out there making things happen. So, throw a little "no" party and revel in your progress. You're doing more than your competitors are likely to be doing, so recognise that! Secondly, each no gets you closer to a 'yes'. By law of averages alone, if you keep going, you're going to get a 'yes'.

By understanding that rejections are not personal and learning from each "no," you've levelled up your sales game like never before. Keep that positive mindset, celebrate your achievements, and go forth fearlessly.

Key takeaways

- You are going to get rejections and 'no's
- It is not personal
- Learn from each 'no' if you can
- Keep a record of objections and brainstorm them
- Pat yourself on the back for doing something rather than nothing!

FREE EXTRA RESOURCES:

To help you out, I have collated some great responses to a "no"– you can download this, free, from https://www.nofluff.biz/spend-less-sell-more or if you can't be bothered typing that in, just scan this QR code.

Chapter 2
Sorry, Divas, It's Not about YOU

Imagine for a moment I'm in your office. (I'm not really there, it's OK. But if I were, I hope there would be coffee and biscuits involved.) So I'm in your office and asking you about your leads. We see you have quite a few in the pipeline, which is fabulous. All of them have been followed up at least once, some of them twice (because you knew I was coming in and would be getting on your case). You are satisfied that you have sent them all the information they could need. And yet here I am, saying, "Let's go again." Are you rolling your eyes at me? Or happy to trust the process?

Nicola: "Time to follow up that lead again!"
Responses I typically hear:

> "I don't want to seem desperate."
> "I don't want to seem pushy."
> "I don't want to seem sleazy."
> "If they're not interested, I'll feel rejected."

"I feel awkward and don't know what to say."

"I don't want to interrupt them if they're busy."

"I feel embarrassed, their enquiry was ages ago."

"I've given them all the information already."

"I don't want to be annoying and risk the relationship."

Notice anything about all of these statements? They all begin with "I". They are all about the salesperson's feelings and mindset, not the reality of the lead's state of mind. How could you presume to know their feelings?

Time to reframe all of this, as I have a newsflash for you; selling is NOT ABOUT YOU. It's not about YOUR feelings and mindset monkeys. Harsh? Don't forget my company is called No Fluff for a reason. But it's said with love. I'll forever be on your side, but however fabulous and wonderful you are, the lead, the prospect, and the client are the focus of your selling efforts.

By poking your head into the cage of these mindset monkeys, you might be projecting your obstacles onto the lead. Your feelings are valid, even if they are holding you back. So, let's try to switch gears and consider a different perspective.

Instead of assuming the lead isn't interested or doesn't want to hear from you, why not entertain the idea that they could be caught up in the whirlwind of life or lost in the Bermuda Triangle of their inbox? Your offer just may not be the most important thing in their world right now. You don't know what is happening.

Don't let your own fears and assumptions cast a shadow over the potential for a fruitful conversation.

Key takeaways

- It's not about YOU

Chapter 3
Mindset Shifting For Sales Success

It's time to reframe those feelings and embrace the opportunity that follow-up presents. Instead of seeing it as a burden, view it as a chance to build relationships, provide value to those who need it, and uncover potential solutions for your leads. Remember, you have a valuable offer that can truly make a difference in their lives or businesses. So, put on your follow-up cape, embrace your role as a helpful guide, and let your enthusiasm and passion shine through. You'll be surprised at the positive responses and connections you can create. Let's conquer those follow-up fears and unlock your true potential!

You might need further convincing. We're talking about overcoming the fear of interrupting, feeling sleazy, and dealing with being "ghosted": all things that we are taught from a young age are baaaad. And this isn't just aimed at the relative newbies to selling and follow up. Around 95% of teams and sales folk I coach are also neglecting their follow up. Luckily, however, this is pretty easily fixed if we have a plan, Stan, which is why you're reading this book. Moreover, rather brilliantly, fixing them shows results fast. This is great, as we need those dopamine hits of success to keep our motivation up.

So, let's look at shifting those limiting beliefs and kicking those mindset monkeys out.

1. Shift: From Interruption to Value Creation

Instead of viewing your follow-up as an interruption to your lead's day, see it as a chance to create value for them instead. You're not bothering them; you're offering solutions and insights that can make a real difference in their lives. When you approach follow-up with the mindset of value creation, you become a trusted problem-solver, not a pesky nuisance. With the Follow-Up Framework that you're going to create using this book, you will see that it is not all about pushing a sale at every turn. Trust the process. Your mission, should you choose to accept it, is to consistently provide valuable content, resources, and solutions in each follow-up interaction. Whether it's sharing industry insights, offering helpful tips, or addressing specific pain points, you need to be a provider of value that your leads can't resist. And don't worry, we don't have to reinvent the wheel with our added-value pieces each time. Don't worry; we will work smart on this. Here's the deal, my fabulous reader: every interaction is a chance to deliver your value and make a lasting impression. If nothing else, each voicemail, email, text or DM you craft in this Follow-Up Framework is a marketing opportunity. Nothing is wasted here. With each interaction, you'll reinforce your expertise and position yourself as their go-to hero. Even if they don't purchase, in their eyes you will remain a source of support and information. That way, you'll be top of their mind for when they are ready to buy.

2. Shift: From Sleaze to Authentic Self

Say goodbye to sleazy vibes, my friends, because authenticity is your secret weapon. Be unapologetically yourself, showcasing your genuine personality and building trust through honest and meaningful connections, and by digging into your empathetic side. One small caveat: we want the "lovely you", not the grumpy-just-woken-up you! We need the "you" that you dig out when at a party, wedding or event! Keep the "moody you" to yourself. When you approach your follow-up with authenticity, your leads will sense it. They'll appreciate your sincerity, and the fear of being perceived as sleazy will fade away like a bad dream. Be confident in who you are, and let your true self shine through.

3. Shift: From Pushy to Persistent

Ah, the art of persistence! It is not the same as pushy. We are going to be the ones who are there, helping them with their decision, understanding their obstacles and objections, mindful of their needs and situations. It's all about understanding the buying journey of your leads. Some will take longer to decide that than others. Some have budgets set at certain times of the year, while others can dip into the coffers at any point. Know your clients. By tailoring your Follow-Up Framework according to your ideal client's buying process, you will convert more of them into clients. Stay committed, my friends, and remember to follow the process.

4. Shift: Rejection to Resilience

"Refuse to attach a negative meaning to the word 'no'. View it as feedback. 'No' tells you to change your approach, create more value, or try again later."

– Anthony Iannarino

As we have discussed, not everyone is going to buy. There are very few businesses that convert at 100%. Or if there are, show me where they are – I want shares. In the world of sales, rejection is part of life. But fear not, brave souls, for rejection is not the end – it's an opportunity for growth. Don't forget our mantra 'It's not personal; it's just a no for now'. I received perhaps 20 offers to subscribe to a TV streaming service before I finally bought it. Now I pay them every month. Embrace rejection as part of the journey to growth and use it to sharpen your skills. Analyse what didn't work, learn from it, and refine your approach. Every rejection brings you closer to a resounding "yes!" Stay resilient, keep your chin up, and let rejection fuel your determination.

I'm going to give you an example of some great follow-up and resilience that I experienced when I was selling my house a few years ago.

I had looked at reviews and information about various estate agents; some were bricks and mortar agencies, others were online only. I checked out their inventory, and asked their commission rates and terms. Three of the local agents came over to value the property and talk me through everything. They were all similar, actually. The online ones gave me their valuation and rates by email; one did it by phone as well.

In the end, I chose one of the local agents. I won't go into his selling techniques here, but he called me the next morning to see if he could help with anything to do with the move, when it happened, such as removal companies in his network. I went with him.

He was busy doing his thing, marketing it and reaching out to his network. I was tied in for around three months before I could co-market or switch agencies. Of the other local agents, only one followed up their visit with a call to see if I wanted to proceed.

This astounds me. Truly my gast is flabbered! Let's look at the effort we'd already expended.

- I had researched their website and marketing, reviews and posts before getting in touch.
- I had enquired and then fixed a time to visit.
- They had driven to the house, spent around 20 minutes with me looking around and given me their valuation and pricing.
- Then… nothing.

After all of that... they didn't follow up. Why not...? I was definitely going to put the house on the market, it was just a question of picking an agent out of several similar offers.

So, the one that bothered following up and was helpful was the one I went with. Bearing in mind each house sold gives them commission, why wouldn't they?

But the story doesn't end there!

Meanwhile, the online estate agency called me back. I said I had decided to go with a local agent and was tied in for a few months. He wished me luck and said he'd be in touch another time.

He sent me an email around a month later, saying he hoped all was going well and with a checklist of things to remember to do when you move house. (That was so handy)!

He called a few weeks after that (about halfway through my contract with the local agent) to see how the viewings were going and if I'd sold yet. I reported back that we hadn't had many viewings, sadly, but I was still tied in. He made a few suggestions to tweak the listing text, which I liked and asked my local agent to make (who was ready to try anything to get the viewers, so made the changes).

At the three-month mark, the digital agency rep called me and asked how it was all going. They asked if I was sick of keeping the house tidy all the time. I liked this touch – it's a common complaint when selling a house that it needs to be neat constantly – especially if you're not naturally a neat freak. Anyway, we had a little chat and I asked about their rates again as my agent hadn't managed to sell the property yet. As you can probably predict, I went with the online agent after my contract finished.

Persistence, added value, and an apparent genuine interest made the deal happen. At no point did I feel harassed, pushed, annoyed, or interrupted.

I hope you have realised by this point that you do not need to be pushy or sleazy to follow-up well. Because here's the truth: it's your job, and yours alone, to follow up on those leadsYes, you heard it right. You're the one who knows the value of your offer. You're the one who wants the business. It's not the lead's duty to come begging at your door, waving their wallets in desperation. Sadly not! Your mission is to take charge, and guide them on their path to purchase if you have a good fit. So, put on your confidence cape, lock those mindset monkeys up and unleash your empathy and charm! Let the world know that you're here to save them from making the wrong choices (or no choices). Remember, you've got the knowledge, the skills, and the determination and soon – the Framework – to make a difference.

Key takeaways

- Add value, genuinely help them on their journey
- Be your fabulous, authentic self to build trust
- Persistence, rather than pushiness
- Build resilience

FREE EXTRA RESOURCES:

If you struggle with getting into the right headspace for selling and are doing everything to put it off, you need my short video to help you move forwards. It's completely free for readers of this book and only takes a few minutes to watch. Go to https://www.nofluff.biz/spend-less-sell-more or if that's too long to type out just scan this QR code to whizz straight there.

Part II
Spend Less

You've already achieved amazing things with your business, offering products or services that leave your customers over the moon. But let's face it, when it comes to sales and marketing, you might not be a "natural". And that's perfectly okay, because there isn't such a thing as a "natural" salesperson who is good at every aspect of selling.

"An important mark of a good leader [is] to know you don't know it all and never will."

– Anne M. Mulcahy

As a wearer of multiple hats and a master of multitasking, you've managed to make impressive sales along the way. However, it's time to take a step back and acknowledge that you may have stumbled upon success rather than executing a well-oiled sales machine. Sure, passion and word-of-mouth referrals have carried you this far, but there's a whole world of untapped potential waiting for you to unleash it – especially if you want to grow further.

In the hustle and bustle of "doing the day job" of delivering your service, it's easy to get swept away by shiny marketing objects and the constant juggling act of emails and social media posts. Just get the leads in, keep getting them in, and by law of averages some of them will buy! Right? Well, yes, but have you considered how much effort and cost you're facing doing that? Is there a better way?

Have you ever stopped to think about the quality of your leads? Probably. You might be frustrated with how many leads head your way and by comparison with how few sales come out the other end. While marketing plays a crucial role in attracting attention, it's the right-fit leads that hold the key to long-lasting customer relationships and jaw-dropping sales conversion rats. And while it would be optimistic to hope every single lead could be converted, let's get that rate up, shall we? Let's unleash the untapped potential hidden within your existing leads.

Throughout this book, we'll equip you with game-changing insights and battle-tested techniques to transform your leads into sales supremos. Say goodbye to relying on sheer luck or random acts of sales brilliance (it's ok to tell everyone that it's just natural talent, even if you know you're using proven processes). It's time to don that sales superhero cape, seize control, harness the full potential of your business, and convert those leads into loyal, paying customers (that bring their friends, too).

Are you ready to shift your focus from spending countless hours and effort on trying to generate new leads to maximising the potential of your existing ones? It's time to unlock the untapped power of your inbox. Together, we're about to reshape your sales approach, optimise your efforts to suit your own business, and set you on a path to exceptional sales growth by converting those prospects you would normally give up on into loyal customers. Get ready to dive in, as I am going to show you not only how to do this, but also why you should bother, I'm going to make it a no-brainer process to follow. You'll walk away with a one page Framework to follow that will make you more money, attract the right-fit clients to your offer, and lower your client acquisition costs. Excited?

Chapter 4
Shiny Marketing Objects

We're in a world where small business owners and entrepreneurs are constantly tempted by shiny marketing objects. These alluring distractions come in various forms, promising endless leads and boundless success. It's like being a kid in a sweet shop, with each new tactic and trend vying for your attention. And I imagine that you are no stranger to the seduction of a new tool, method or program that will teach you "sales"" but in reality is more focused on lead generation or branding. These have their place but in practice, they can simply divert your focus from doing the sales work on existing leads.In fact – a personal peeve of mine is when marketing gurus say they'll make you more sales – when in fact they'll get you great leads. The sales work is done after the lead is in. Great ads alone don't make sales (well, particularly for services). Anyway – I'll gently climb down off my soapbox now.

But here is the thing: while more leads are always desirable, there's a hidden secret that many overlook. By focusing on converting and following up with the leads you already have, you can save an incredible amount of time, money, and effort. It's time to discover the real goldmine within your existing leads.

I get it – the pursuit of more leads seems like a never-ending adventure. It's exciting. You want to be using the latest tech and techniques. You have massive FOMO. You're worried that if you don't try the latest thing, your competitors will scoop up all the booty. It's easy to fall into the trap of thinking that the solution lies in constantly acquiring new prospects. But let's pause for a moment and reflect. What if, instead of chasing after every shiny marketing promise, you redirected more of your energy towards converting and nurturing the leads you already have? The prospects you've already met? Future buyers that just need an extra nudge. It's like realising you have a treasure trove right at your fingertips.

And before any marketers reading this throw the book down in disgust, I am not saying we should ditch lead generation. Not at all. We will always need fresh leads, However, by attracting the right leads into the pipeline in the first place, then by qualifying early to make sure there's a "fit", and nurturing those with care and attention rather than letting it slide if they're not biting our hands off, then we will convert more of them into buyers.

You don't need tons more leads.

You need to work smarter on the ones you already have.

Just imagine the possibilities. By channelling your efforts into converting and following up with your existing leads, you can transform them into loyal customers. These leads are not mere numbers; they are potential champions of your brand. Through effective follow-up strategies, you can build relationships, address their needs, and guide them toward making a purchase with ease. Even if they don't buy straight away, I will show you how to maintain engagement, hopefully without you rolling your eyes at me. It's like turning coal into diamonds, but without all the pressure. And you can do it on autopilot. We just need to make a plan. Which is why you're here, so that's handy.

Right, so what happens if you don't follow up and nurture more? What happens if you do a few follow-ups, they're ghosting you, and you think they're a chilly lead as you have other things to do? When you fail to follow up correctly, as the phrase goes, you're essentially "leaving money on the table". Think about it – you've invested time, money, and resources into acquiring those leads. Each lead represents a potential sale, a chance to grow your business. Cash to buy that yacht with. By neglecting them, you're not only wasting the resources you have already invested in lead generation, but also missing out on the revenue they could bring in. It's time to put an end to this costly oversight.

Yes, some leads are duds. Maybe they're just browsing, or they're not a good fit. Of course they won't all convert. But more of them will once you have a Follow-Up Framework. By focusing on the fortune that is already IN your world of leads, you'll find the ones that are a good fit, increase that conversion rate (which will increase revenue), and reduce your cost-per-lead. This will mean you don't need to spend so much cash and time on lead generation. And of course you will become super-efficient and be able to do a little smug dance. All good news!

Now, I know what you're thinking – isn't follow up a bit like nagging? Can't it be too pushy or awkward? Fear not, I've got you! I'm here to show you the magical ways of nurturing without being overbearing – and without having to get all caught up in your head about whether you're being creepy or not. Get ready to sprinkle stardust and add value at every turn, so your leads will be charmed and captivated.

I won't sugarcoat it – follow up can be a challenge if you don't have a plan. It requires time, a little more effort, and a sprinkle of organisation. But don't you worry! With the right approach, armed with your own Follow-Up Framework, which we are going to make together, you can conquer this challenge and unlock its true potential. Effective follow up is about building trust, nurturing relationships, and providing the information your leads need to make an informed decision. It's like a dance, where you lead them gracefully towards becoming loyal customers. And it should feel like a dance too; whether it's a tango, waltz or jive depends on your personal preference – the dance is all about you and the prospect. You don't leave them hanging at the side of the dancefloor wondering if you'll ever ask them to boogie or not (and then wandering off and dancing with your competitor).

I'm going to give you an example.

Case Study: James and the Giant Deal.

> A group of friendly competing companies in a marketing group of language schools in the UK are emailed a hot lead from the group's HQ. Around ten providers of a matching service within the marketing group receive the lead's request for information.
>
> All ten reply. After all, they want the business, they are polite, and they know about responding to requests, so they fire off their emails.
>
> However, James, the one that I coached, has a Follow-Up Framework. He picks up the phone immediately upon receiving the request and calls the lead. He knows that the enquiry is now probably a few hours old as it has come via the group, but still – the plan is kicking in!
>
> It is written there, in his Framework, to call within five

minutes for his first follow up. Not only does James know that speed of response to that initial enquiry is game-changing, he also loves a bit of friendly competition. He wants to win the deal over his competitors, much though he loves them all. Business is business and he wants the sale. It's also a great potential gateway, as he doesn't have as much of a foothold in that lead's country as he'd like. Plus he knows that, if he can pull this off, and deliver a great service, this lead will become a fan, who will rebook with him and not bother going to any competitors next time. He's not making one sale, he's establishing a foundation for future sales from the same lead. Time to show this lovely lead how much his business is valued by James and how efficient and attentive James can be.

They have a brief chat, in which the lead is taken aback to have been approached directly by phone, and pleasantly surprised by the swift care and attention. They swap WhatsApp numbers and James sends the information and quote through as soon as he hangs up, as promised. He also connects with him on social media and diligently loads the information up on his CRM.

The story doesn't end there, though. James is armed with the Follow-Up Framework that we went through.

Having sent the email outlining the quote. He gives it a few hours and sends a friendly WhatsApp to say it was lovely to chat and the quote should be in the lead's inbox . He also says he'll call back the next day to go over details and any questions the lead may have. He suggests a time.

The lead WhatsApps back and agrees the time suits him and he'll check the email now.

The next day arrives, and James duly calls the lead. There's no answer, which is a bit annoying, but you never know what is happening behind the scenes. So he hangs up and tries again half an hour later than agreed but still no answer. So, James pops onto the lead's social media, likes a few posts, and comments on one of them. He logs his attempts to reach the lead onto his database notes.

No answer again, so he sends a WhatsApp message to explain he called, he's happy to catch up later on that day, he's free between x and y and, by the way, did the lead know that they had five star results in their recent accreditation report? The lead's clients will be assured of such a great service and James can't wait to look after them.

That time comes and goes. James then sends a quick voice note hoping everything is OK and explains he'll whizz over his diary link so the lead can pick a time that suits him, but if not, he'll try again the next day.

Nothing. Zip.

By this time, James is worried a competitor has got to the lead. Their emails may all have arrived by now. He could have been undercut on price or outsold on other features. But he doesn't know for sure. He starts to lose hope slightly, as the initial excitement and competitive spirit has now dimmed a little. He may even be a bit sulky about it, if he were being honest. But, he remembers our work together and trusts the process, and goes back to his Follow-Up Framework, while swearing at me under his breath.

The next day comes and he calls the lead again. No answer. So he sends a quick email with some tips that the lead would find useful about the service. James is a bit worried the lead is going cold as time goes on. Before his coaching with me started, he would have given up long ago. Probably after the lead had stood him up that first time.Later that day, James tries to call again. BINGO! He gets through. The lead doesn't explain why he wasn't answering or hadn't shown up, but letting bygones be bygones, and fired up again James moves forward; they have a bit of a natter and then get down to negotiating on the deal. A few details need to be changed so the quote is amended and sent through.

James then sends a video over WhatsApp on his morning walk showing the route his students take overlooking the water (nicely demonstrating the location of his school) in which he explains that he'll call the lead back later that day so they can get started on implementation.

The lead sends a video back of his morning walk too, laughing, as the weather is better with him than it was with James in the UK. He agrees they'll talk and arranges a time.

When the time comes, they switch to Zoom and finalise the deal.

The lead is a reseller, offering James' services to his local clients, and in return receiving commission. This is a small cost for James to swallow in exchange for signing up a group of paying students to his language school.

And with some ongoing nurturing and follow-up of this lead (now a client) he'll receive more groups, time and time again.

Ask yourself, if you'd been in this position, when would you have let it go? After the lead didn't show up the first time? Second time? You wouldn't be alone. Most salesfolk give up after just the second follow up.

If we were to map this process out for James as it happened, it would look like this:

- inbound lead
- five minutes - respond by phone
- immediately - follow up with an emailed quote, and connect on social media
- three hours later – WhatsApp
- one day later – phone call no answer – WhatsApp message and socials interaction
- a few hours later WhatsApp voice note and interesting fact
- the next day – call, then email with tips
- later that day – call again and email new quote
- the next day -WhatsApp video note
- the same day – call arranged, deal comes in

By contrast, this is what probably happened at most of the other language schools who received the lead.

- inbound lead
- within 24 hours email quote sent to lead
- two days later - email re-sent to see if lead has any questions and an offer to have a zoom chat
- no reply – then perhaps a phone call if they're keen and don't have too many meetings that day
- otherwise – assumed cold/uninterested and left

If this sounds like what you would do in this situation, this is entirely normal. No judgement from me – but frankly, my lovely, we can do better. That's why you're here, reading this book. How about we make this one-page plan that should not take tons of effort to follow but that means you have a fighting chance to convert this lead and all those like it?

Key takeaways

- Spend on generating the RIGHT leadsOr don't spend on lead generation if you're not prepared to do the follow-up
- Speed of response is important
- Personal connection and persistence works wonders
- Resilience in the face of 'no reply' works
- Follow-up gets you the deals.

FREE EXTRA RESOURCES:

In this case study James builds rapport quickly and in different ways. Rapport building takes practice and a dash of resilience. I have more materials for you on this that I couldn't fit into this book – totally free, you can get the fast guide 'Questions To Ask To Build Rapport'

Just go to this link or scan the QR code for the complete list of extra materials for this book: https://www.nofluff.biz/spend-less-sell-more

Chapter 5
The Buyer Journey and Hesitations

The journey isn't always just a straightforward march through all of your steps towards the sale; it's a dynamic voyage shaped by emotions, information, and personal experiences, each of which has a different duration in each of the steps, and is influenced by a myriad of factors. Some go backwards before they go forwards towards the sale. This doesn't make our lives easier, right? I mean, why can't they just see how fabulous we are and simply buy?! Sadly, it mostly doesn't work like that. But we can do our utmost to help as many buyers as possible make it over the finish line.

Let me make it clear upfront (just in case you were in doubt): I'm no brain scientist, neuropsychologist, or expert in any brain-related field. So, if what I share here sparks your curiosity, I encourage you to delve deeper with your own research. The neuro-marketing field is fascinating and there are some brilliant studies being done. I'd expect to see more of the results hitting the mainstream. What I have learned, however, is that decision-making in the buying process delves into the depths of our minds, and comes into play even before we consciously recognize the need to make a decision.

The brain's limbic system (or Reptilian Brain) is a critical player at the helm. It's the domain of emotions, and it significantly influences the way individuals perceive, interpret, and make decisions about products and services. This system weaves our past experiences and memories into the tapestry of every choice we make.

When a prospect encounters a product or service, or even a salesperson, their "old" brain first assesses the likelihood of danger – this is a fight, flight or freeze response. We do this automatically – you won't usually be aware it is happening. However, let's assume you don't come across like an axe murderer or scary lion, so we manage to get past the Reptilian Brain section.At this point, their brain's limbic system draws upon previous encounters to guide their response. Positive experiences foster an inclination towards engagement, while negative ones lead to scepticism. This mechanism, largely driven by emotions, can either fuel hesitations or alleviate them. If they have been annoyed by, or – worse – tricked by a salesperson before, they will have a negative reception if you come across as "salesy". This is the main reason why "sales" has a bad reputation – we focus on the sleazy salesfolk we have come across (often many years ago) and those we see on films such as *The Wolf of Wall Street*. If they have had a bad experience, it will be stored in the limbic system and it's up to you to get past it. Don't worry, I've got your back on this and we'll work on it!Think of the limbic system as your brain's unique library, meticulously storing memories of your interactions with different products and services. Each time you present your offering, the brain summons this library, cross-referencing it with the present encounter.

If a past experience was positive, the prospect may lean towards a favourable perception. However, if prior engagement resulted in doubts or frustrations, those hesitations could surface.

It's only after our limbic system has weighed in with a decision (before you are even aware you're making a decision, remember), that your more logical brain cranks into action. The neocortex is the logical, reasoning part that will look at facts, figures and reasoning. However, the brain has already pretty much made up its mind, so to speak, as buying decisions are predominantly made on emotion.Let's explore a few relatable examples.

Example 1:

I like chocolate. I particularly like Cadbury's Chocolate Buttons. I associate them with fond memories from my childhood, when we used to stay with my lovely aunt in the summer and she used to give us treat packets of Buttons if we'd been good. Being good usually involved simply staying out of her way, and helping with the cleaning in her job at the local bingo hall. (Side note...the stuff we used to find left behind! Not just dabbers, umbrellas and glasses, but actual 50p pieces (booty, yay!), and once a prosthetic leg, which raised all sorts of questions about how they had left the place without it). But anyway, back to Buttons. We used to have treat bags on birthdays and they generally featured in celebratory moments. Over the years, they have become intertwined with feelings of being treasured, of comfort, nostalgia, treats and happiness in my mind.

One day, I came across a new brand of chocolate, Hershey's, that I hadn't tried before. Despite hearing positive reviews about its taste and quality, with my American cousins raving about it, I found myself hesitating to give it a try. Strange. It was chocolate, it is likely to be good, and even if it weren't, how bad an experience could eating chocolate be? Why was I hesitating? Unconsciously, my limbic system was at play. The brand I had grown up with was not just a product; it was (and still is) tied to my emotions and memories. My limbic system was reacting to this new option as a potential threat to positive associations with my favourite brand. As a result, I felt a sense of reluctance about trying the new chocolate, even if logically it might have been just as good or even better.

This simple example showcases how the limbic system's influence can extend beyond rational thinking (I mean, come on Nicola – it's chocolate! Eat it!) Emotions and past experiences deeply shape our perceptions, preferences, and decisions, often guiding us in ways we might not be consciously aware of.

Let's try an example from business I recently witnessed.

Example 2:

I was in an education agency office, working with their team, and we had some virtual meetings set up with two prospective educator partners. This agency recruits around 100 students into boarding schools per year, each of which is "worth" £30,000 per year to a school. It's not all about the money, of course; the child always comes first, otherwise the agency would be out of business in no time, but we were focusing on revenue for the moment. The schools would like this agent to represent and market them to prospective parents and pupils. Times were hard, and domestic recruitment was down, so they needed to increase international recruitment. For each new agent who would represent them, they could count on several new pupils, year on year. The schools were fairly similar in size, academic achievement, facilities etcetera. So it was unlikely the agent would take on both schools.

So, we set up a duel and decided to have an arm wrestling contest to decide the winning school to be represented... OK, not really. The agency team sat and listened carefully to each of the school representatives in order to make informed decisions that involve no physical combat.

School A provided a comprehensive presentation that highlighted their expertise, rankings, facilities, pastoral care, awards, nationality mix of international students and boarding house photos. Truly, this was is beautiful. It had impressive data. However, during their presentation, the School's Admissions Officer focused on facts and figures. He emphasised the impressive facilities and data on past results.

School B also presented facts and figures but took a different approach. During the presentation, the speaker not only presented their facilities and rankings but also took the time to connect on a personal level. He shared success stories of similar agencies they had worked with and their clients, demonstrating empathy for the challenges the agency faced every day in counselling parents and children. He highlighted exactly how their team would help and support challenges the agency faced, and also how they would ensure the pupils were happy (not just achieving). He also stressed that this could help the agency with their word-of-mouth-recommendations. Frankly, by the end of this I was ready to take their team. I was fully invested. The agent also felt understood and valued.

In this scenario, the limbic system came into play. The agent's brain processed the emotional connection created by School B's approach. The personal touch triggered positive emotions, such as a sense of being valued, understood, and supported. This emotional connection activated the limbic system, and thus influenced the agent's perception of both schools.

The emotional connection created a positive association, leading the agent to feel that School B truly understood their needs and cared about their success, as well as the success of the students. This emotional influence ultimately swayed the decision-making process, leading the agent to choose School B over School A.

Understanding this aspect of the buyer journey empowers you with the Jedi-like ability to tackle hesitations and empathise with the leads who have chosen to enquire about your services. When a potential customer hesitates, it's not just about the here and now – it's a culmination of all their previous interactions with the universe. And sometimes it's about their expectations of the future. It is up to you to build a foundation, with positive interactions.

The limbic system, acting like a wise old owl, connects the dots between past encounters and future decisions. To make progress, you've got a dual mission: first, to nurture positive vibes, trust and rapport, and second, to show off your superhero skills in addressing past concerns and objections. By doing this, you're not only calming current qualms but also shaping the prospect's view of future engagements. You need, in short, to appeal to, and perhaps appease the emotional part of their brains, before you wow them with your logic.

So, as you navigate the thrilling maze of the buyer journey, bear in mind that it's not just about the immediate action. It's about each and every touchpoint playing a part in crafting the prospect's overall perception. Leveraging the power of the limbic system is the key to positioning yourself as a reliable and trusted solution over several touchpoints.

Key takeaways

- Use emotion first, then features to work with the brain
- Show empathy with the prospect's own life/business/needs
- Relevant stories trigger the emotional buy-in of prospects
- It's not about YOU.

FREE EXTRA RESOURCES:

These touchpoints give you opportunities for what are called "micro conversions". Really, these are mini "closes" along the way that help move a prospect onwards and upwards. I have created a free extra section on micro conversions for you, explaining what they are, and how to incorporate them into your selling. Head to https://www.nofluff.biz/spend-less-sell-more to get this bonus section, no charge (or just scan this QR code).

Chapter 6
Spending Less by Converting More

Still not convinced? Or do you need some facts and figures before you commit to making your Follow-Up Framework?

Alright then, let's dive into the serious statistical stuff so I can show you WHY developing your Follow-Up Framework is going to stop you spending so much on your lead generation and shiny marketing temptations.

Companies that excel at lead nurturing generate 50% more sales-ready leads at 33% lower cost.

(Source: Forrester Research) [6:1]

Now, if that's not magic, I don't know what is! You save money. You make more sales. Or at least, with this statistic, you generate 50% more sales-ready leads – so it's up to you to get them over the line, but you generate 50% more leads that are primed to purchase, making the odds of closing them significantly higher. This is great news! Less cash splashed on lead generation to get to the same revenue goals – whoop!

Nurtured leads make 47% larger purchases than non-nurtured leads.

(Source: The Annuitas Group) [6:1]

Ooh. That's exciting – not only will your Follow-Up Framework help you save money, and make more sales, but, according to The Annuitas Group, those lovely leads will also make larger sales! You'll see for yourself that, when trust is increased through your nurturing follow-up, they spend more.

But don't count your pennies yet; this extra spend doesn't come from thin air. It's a result of your follow-up efforts, during which you sprinkle your wisdom and expertise into touchpoints along their journey. You guide them with care, offering valuable insights and tailored solutions, and in return, they reward you with their loyalty and their wallets.

60% of customers say no four times before saying yes.

(Source: Invesp) [6:2]

Ah, the "no" again – a word that can evoke a whirlwind of emotions in even the most seasoned sales professionals. When a potential customer says "no," it can feel like a personal blow, leaving you grappling with a sense of rejection and self-doubt. In fact, it is this fear of rejection that can prevent you from even trying to follow up in the first place.

This also explains why many people are reluctant to make sales calls; instead they send email after email. You can't hear "no" from an email, you just don't hear back and that isn't as confrontational as a direct "no thanks" on the phone. You may feel that if they haven't jumped on the opportunity to buy from you, then they are not interested. And with each time they fail to reply, you believe the likelihood that they're not keen is even higher. But this statistic shows otherwise. They are likely to say "no" four times before saying yes. There is hope! You just need a little more grit and persistence, together with a cunningly timed plan.

However, if they have said "no" to you once, the fear of being perceived as pushy or intrusive looms large, causing some to hesitate in their follow-up efforts. But let me share a little secret with you – the power of a well-crafted Follow-Up Framework works wonders here. Remember that? That's why you're here. We will make this beautiful Framework that will allow the lead to feel nurtured, informed, and valued.

50% of leads are qualified but not yet ready to buy.

(Source: Gleanster Research) [6:1]

What does that actually mean? Well, it means that these leads meet your criteria for being, you know, a GOOD lead. They have the cash. They have a problem you can solve. They have the decision maker's buy-in. But they aren't ready to buy YET. It's not a "no" forever, it's a "no for now". It is simply sensible to follow them up until they are ready. You want to be the one they go to when they're raring to go, right? Then you need to schedule the follow ups. Simple.

The beauty of this master Follow-Up Framework is that your leads won't even realise they're part of it. Instead of feeling like pawns in a sales game, they'll perceive your interactions as authentic and valuable. And in fact, if you are passionate about your solutions, you will authentically be adding value to them. I will be showing you how. Your follow up will transcend mere persistence; it will embody a genuine desire to assist and provide solutions. And that makes you a fabulous person. Even if it ends in a "no", they are still going to recommend you, refer you and follow you.

More about rejection in a little while but let's crack on with our statistics to show you how important follow up is.

It takes eight touches to convert a lead, or five touches for top performers. So… not the one or two follow-ups that you've probably been making so far.

According to sales guru Grant Cardone, while only 10% of salespeople make more than three contacts, 90% of sales are made after that contact. In fact, 10% of sales are made after the fourth, and a massive 80% of sales are made on the fifth to twelfth contact.

Mind blown? I hope so, as this goes to show that the one or two follow ups that are sitting nicely in your comfort zone right now are just not enough to convert the number of leads into sales that you could be doing, if only you made more points of contact.

And I get it, I really do, reaching out again and again has always seemed embarrassing to you, but this book is about to show you what to do, and when, how and what happens next. I'm going to make it as easy as possible for you. I'm going to walk you through the process of making this Follow-Up Framework, we're going to design it fabulously to fit yourself and your ideal client avatar and you're going to start converting more leads into bookings. You won't have to cringe. You will know you're adding value to these leads, whether they buy or not. And you're going to see how many more leads would have got away!

"Sales is about actions: The more you do, the more you get! Consistency is the key to success."

– Iulia Neicovcean

Key takeaways

- Nurture leads well, they'll spend more, at a lower cost of acquisition.
- Leads nurtured spend more than those that aren't.
- Leads will say no before they say yes.
- Half of leads aren't ready to buy YET.
- You need five to twelve touches to convert a lead.
- You aren't likely to be doing more than two or three currently.

Chapter 7
Finding the Perfect Fit

Imagine you're a treasure hunter exploring a vast, uncharted island in search of valuable artefacts. You have limited time and supplies to uncover hidden gems, and you can only carry a certain amount, as you brought along the wrong bag – so you need to be strategic. You have an old, yellowing map in your hand and you know certain artefacts will make you your fortune are likely to be there.

As you navigate through dense forests and scale towering cliffs, you don't dig randomly or collect any trinkets you stumble upon. Instead, you rely on your map, instincts and knowledge to pinpoint the area likely to hold the most precious treasures – the ones that align perfectly with your mission.

By focusing your efforts on those specific spots, you maximise your chances of discovering those rare and valuable artefacts while optimising your limited resources. You get to where "X" marks the spot and you pick and choose the trinkets and artefacts that you believe are going to be the most valuable. If you try to carry all of them, you will be risking dropping the most precious cargo.

In the world of business, and especially sales within a business, finding the right-fit leads for your business follows a similar principle. Just like a treasure hunter, you want to invest your time and resources in pursuing those leads that are most likely to yield valuable results. By targeting those who align with your business values, needs, and offerings (and, shall we be frank – those who have the budget), you increase your chances of striking gold – and will more easily convert these leads into loyal customers. In the world of sales, we refer to these ideal customers as "ideal client avatars." They could also be known as "buyer personas", "ideal client personas" or "buyer types". Whatever you want to call them, they're the ideal representation of your dream customers, embodying the qualities of your most valuable, satisfied clients. These are the folks who not only appreciate the value you are offering but also align with your business values, becoming long-term supporters.

Now, you might be wondering, "Why is it so important to identify my ideal client avatar?" Great question! Imagine throwing your limited budget and precious time into pursuing leads that just don't click with your business. It's like trying to sell snow to a polar bear – a chilly endeavour that leaves you feeling chilly and drains your resources. And it's not just your resources, but also your motivation and belief in yourself! By focusing your efforts on attracting and nurturing the right-fit leads, you're setting yourself up for success.

Frankly, everything starts with the customer. They will only buy if you solve a pain point they have. Often, we are asked to sell a product or a service to clients but not told what outcomes that client could expect, what worries we could help them allay, what dreams we could help them reach. We revert back to what suits US. What WE want. When in fact, it always starts with what the right-fit buyers want, need and will pay for.Often when I go into businesses, or am asked to train teams, I simply won't do it if they haven't completed the ideal client avatar work (and included emotional buying drivers). There are plenty of sales coaches and trainers that will – but I have the luxury of choice, and I don't want to just tick a 'sales training' box, I want the work I do with that team to help not only the salesfolk hit targets, but their prospects to feel understood and able to buy more easily, AND then go away to become raving fans. And I would question why any business wouldn't want to understand their prospective clients better.

As a small business with limited resources, you know that every penny and minute counts. So that might be why you skip the ideal client part. I understand why it's crucial to make the most of your budget and time. But by honing in on your ideal client avatar, you can ensure that your marketing and sales efforts are directed toward those individuals who are most likely to become your fiercely loyal customers.

Think about it – by serving your ideal client avatar, you'll not only skyrocket your sales conversion rates but also enhance customer satisfaction and retention. It's like unlocking that treasure chest of success that allows you to maximise your resources and achieve higher sales results.

Now, crafting your ideal client avatar doesn't require a magic wand or a crystal ball (though if you have them handy, I'm all for accessorising). It's about getting to know your most valuable customers and what makes them tick. Start by asking yourself some questions:

- Who are your most satisfied and loyal customers? The ones who can't stop raving about your business?
- What are their demographics, such as age, gender, location, and occupation?
- What are their challenges and pain points that your business has the power to solve?

- What dreams, desires, and aspirations do they hold dear?
- Where do they hang out online and offline, ready to discover their next favourite thing?

As you answer these questions, you'll uncover the secrets to your ideal client avatar. This knowledge will guide your marketing and sales efforts, allowing you to craft messages that resonate, choose the right platforms through which to connect, and create irresistible offers that make them say, "Sign me up!"

I find it works well to craft my ideal client avatar away from my desk and usual surroundings. There, I am "me". I have notifications popping up. The dog wants to go out. I have a list of things to do that can keep me within my regular role. But I need to delve into the mind of someone else, my ideal client, so I go where they might go and do this work. For example, if they are someone that might like an artsy café, I'll find one and embrace their environment. If they are more of a posh hotel type I'll pay for that expensive coffee and sit there to do this. I always relax before this exercise, then I close my eyes and imagine I AM the ideal client. What would I be feeling, worrying about, or hoping for? I suspect the staff think I'm a very strange fish as I sit there with a notebook closing my eyes and mumbling. But never mind!

Remember, your ideal client avatar is not a static concept. It's a vibrant representation of your most valuable customers, and it will evolve and grow as your business does. By regularly revisiting and refining your ideal client avatar, you'll ensure that your sales strategies remain as dynamic and exciting as your target audience.

You may also have more than one – you may work with businesses, but also directly with consumers. In which case, craft one of each. But only do one at a time; completely immerse yourself in one avatar, and their needs and wants and worries and dreams. Only after you've done that should you work on the next.

Key takeaways

- Do the background work on your Ideal Client Avatars
- Ensure this includes emotions
- Approach it from their perspective, don't force it to fit what you're selling
- Remember their journey doesn't end after your service, what will they do with it to enhance their lives
- It's all about THEM.

FREE EXTRA RESOURCES:

If you'd like a downloadable and printable template you can use to create your ideal client avatars, you can grab a free basic one from my extra resources page https://www.nofluff.biz/spend-less-sell-more Perfect to take to the café and complete, or to have a go in your team. Or scan the QR code to save the typing!

Section: 7:1
Establishing "Right Fit" Early

Now that you've unlocked the secrets of your ideal client avatars and have them in your sights, you're practically a mind-reader. You know what makes them tick, what gives them goosebumps, and what makes them want to hit that "Buy Now" button. You've got the inside scoop on their favourite chat and the last thing they binge-watched on Netflix. When you talk to them, they should be feeling that you understand them as if you've been friends for life. These avatars are more real to you than ever, and you're ready to welcome them with open arms.

But hold on a minute! Not every lead who stumbles into your orbit is going to be a perfect fit. Sure, it'd be fantastic to shower your attention on every single one, but let's be real – you're not made of time and money. You're on a mission to spend less and sell more, remember, so it's time to be a little more selective. It's time for you to unleash the power of lead qualification.

Gosh, that sounds dull, doesn't it? But lead qualification is your new best friend. The earlier you can qualify a lead as being likely to be a good fit, or (just as importantly) to NOT be a good fit – the more time you save. So, it's time to brush up on how we can do this.

Now, before I dive headfirst into the wild and fluffy world of sales and marketing, let's take a breath and slow things down. Whether you're a seasoned pro or just starting out, it's important to take a step back and make sure you're not wasting your precious time on leads we don't have the potential to become customers. Trust me, I've seen the rabbit holes, and they're not as thrilling as they sound.

Lead qualification is like playing Cupid – you're pairing your product or service with the perfect match. It's about distinguishing the hot prospects from the lukewarm ones, so you can focus your attention where it counts. In this chapter, I'm going to break it all down, strip away the fluff, and show you how to separate the gold nuggets from the time-drainers.

It may be that you don't actually have many leads. In this case – work your magic on the leads you do have and become a sales sleuth – why are some of them buying, and some of them not buying? Get curious – even if you're downhearted that someone didn't purchase, use the opportunity to ask some great questions about what they DO want, and what they WOULD buy, what their real issues are, and what is really standing in their way. This will help you refine your ideal client avatar even further, and also your offer and your marketing strategy. But – this book isn't about lead generation (though the avatar work will help you with that). This book is about converting more of the leads you have into customers as efficiently as possible. So once you have the right kind of leads coming in, then what?

NOTE: when you attract a lead, you are going to need some basic information from them, aside from finding out what they need or want and whether you can help them. You're going to need to capture some details from them that will enable you to use the one page Follow-Up Framework we're going to be making later in the book. You'll probably have a form to fill in, or your own way of recording data. And this might include all sorts of questions that you need answered before you follow up with them, especially if it's a complex product or service. But as a basic guide you're going to need the following in order to nurture them through your process:

- name
- email
- phone number/WhatsApp

If you have an enquiry form – these are obligatory. Even so, they may just make up a phone number, but it's worth including.

OK, so the web form is sorted out and you've ensured you're capturing the data you're going to need later? Fabulous! Let's crack on then.

Are you ready to dive into the world of lead qualification? Brace yourself for some acronyms that will make your head spin with excitement! We've got MQLs, SQLs, and PQLs – marketing qualified leads, sales qualified leads, and product qualified leads. These terms might sound fancy, but here's a little secret: companies around the world often have different opinions on the exact criteria for each. I once witnessed a heated debate between a Marketing Manager and a Sales Manager in a boardroom; they were arguing about what constituted a "Marketing Qualified Lead" as opposed to a "Sales Qualified Lead." Notepads were slammed on the table. Pens were pointed. Whiteboard flow charts were involved. But let's not stress over these fine details. After all, you're not Apple or ICI – you're a small business owner trying to make sense of your own leads. So, let's keep it simple, shall we?

Really, all we are doing is making sure the leads we have are likely to be a good fit for what we offer. That's it. We need to check to see if we are:

a) attracting the right ideal client avatars to approach (if you must – Marketing Qualified Leads).

b) checking, usually in a more personalised way, if they are likely to buy (if we really need to label it, Sales Qualified Leads).

c) noticing if they have interacted with our service or product before in some way. (This is often the overlooked one, a Product Qualified Lead). They have already experienced the product or service, for example, they have had a tester product or taster session.

We simply need to work out what makes one person more likely to travel with us to a purchase than another. We won't always get this right, either. We are using our "best guess" here. And, as we have a safe space here in which to discuss these things, you're going to mess it up. You're not always going to be right. Which is a shocker if you're the Big Cheese and supposed to know everything.

Sometimes you'll have thought a lead wasn't a good fit, but they then purchase and become a fantastic client. And others time, you'll think they're oven-ready for your offer, literally tailor-made to be your perfect fit, and then they end up not buying and you're left rocking in a corner with some ice cream pondering your life choices.

If that is you, get up, dust yourself off and keep going!

So, enough with acronyms already! MQLs, SQLs, PQLs – they're all ways to qualify a lead.

Now we need to check what makes a good lead for YOU and your business. Why not get down the nitty gritty and make a checklist of what would make a good customer? This doesn't just mean their characteristics from the ideal client avatar work, but the practical stuff too.

There are usually some general checks you can make to see if someone is qualified or not, but as it's your own business, and you know it best, you will probably want to add your own. This is especially true if you have a more nuanced sale, with complex options involving multiple departments and decision makers.

Some of these qualifying checks may not be discoverable until you are further into conversations, especially if you have a complex process to determine their needs – but the earlier you can find out about them, the less time you will spend on those that are not willing, or cannot purchase.

CASE STUDY: Alice in Fund-less land

A wonderful life coach I worked with, Alice, was spending a lot of time on discovery calls, and not enough of them were converting into paying clients. When we looked into this a little more, we could see two main problems. One was about her qualifying process, and the other was that she was giving away so much value in her discovery calls that there was no real need to purchase.

The main problem from a sales point of view was that she wasn't qualifying them early enough in the process, so she was giving everyone a free discovery call, an hour at a time, and by the end still wasn't sure if they had the ability or desire to purchase further sessions. She was pretty sure they had the desire to – but desire alone does not a customer make.

Qualifying early on was key to saving hours and hours of time. But how, when it's all a bit awkward asking about money and if they're committed? I could see this client cringe when I talked to her about it. So we needed a way for her to feel comfortable about qualifying her leads.

Firstly we cut the discovery call to 30 minutes maximum. This was the first stage actually, and she is now doing 15 minute calls – go her! Let's stop giving our time away for free if it is not necessary.

Secondly, when the appointment scheduler (Calendly in this case) was sent out she enabled the questions feature. This set the call up but allowed her to find out early on if they had some of the criteria needed. She wasn't ready to refuse any calls based on these criteria, but you could if you're able to (or brave enough).

Thirdly, she put the price range of her services in the blurb on her appointment setter so they were coming into the call with an idea of budget. She also included a section so they could note their goals for any life coaching they might book with her after the discovery call. And finally, she included a question about when the client was looking to start coaching, should they find her a good fit. They were not all obligatory questions but they readied the client for the call.

She was also concerned that she was missing potential leads, but, as her conversion from discovery call through to paying client tripled within six months, she was saving time by not giving her fabulousness away for free. She was also talking to prepared, engaged people on those calls, which made converting them into wonderful, great-fit clients much easier, and off they went into their journey together.

Section 7.2
Finding your Right Fit

"Every sale has five basic obstacles: no need, no money, no hurry, no desire, no trust."

– Zig Ziglar

So, what are your criteria for qualifying a good lead: a good fit for your business?

As Zig pointed out, we need to check our lead has a need for what we are offering, has the money to afford it, has urgency or a timeline in mind, has a desire for it, and trusts us to supply it.

I'm going to chuck another acronym at you here, as it can be handy: BANT. It is a good start for a qualifying checklist:

- Budget – are they likely to have the cash for what you are offering?
- Authority – are they the decision maker? Or one of the decision makers?
- Need – do their needs align with what you are offering?
- Time – does their timeline for making a decision work with your offer?

And outside of BANT here are some more; just pick and choose your criteria -these are YOUR ideal clients!

- Ready – are they ready to engage and work with you/ purchase from you?
- Do they trust you enough to deliver what they need and want?

- Do they need to try something first (a tester, taster or similar)?
- Do you need to find anything else out first (for instance, do they have the right systems/set-up for your solution, and are they in the right area/country)?

Now, it's time for you to develop your own checklist to qualify leads. Don't worry if you can't find out all the answers in your first interaction with them; building trust, learning their needs, and establishing rapport are all also important in the early stages – but aim to qualify as early as possible, as that, my friend, is what will help you save time, money and effort.

Right! So, make a list of a maximum of six qualifying criteria. Do it now! Boil it down, and don't get too wordy.

My qualifying criteria might be:

- they have a small business that needs sales support (need)
- they have proven services/products already
- they have a budget of £x to invest in sales improvement (budget)
- the owner or sales leader is onboard (authority)
- they're aware of timelines for working with me and want to start by XX (timeline)
- we like each other (at least on first impressions!)

I also have a list of criteria that would DISqualify them! I know – it seems cruel. But it's just as important to define who isn't a good fit, so you don't waste your energy. They may become a good fit later on – so we keep in touch – just not as intensively. You may not want to disqualify anyone, and it might be that everyone is a good fit, or can purchase your product. In which case, skip this list! However, usually there is at least one (albeit they need to be over or under a certain age to purchase).

For me, if a lead meets all of my qualifying criteria but also any of the following apply, I disqualify them. Now, please remember this is my own business and I have built it in my own way. I work with small to medium sized businesses, often in education. The ways I work with clients range from a low-touch, group membership of my sales coaching; my signature Accelerator program which is one-to-one coaching for three months; and then into my high-touch consultancy establishing a sales function from scratch and then coaching the leader and team in best use of the tools and actions. Each would have slightly different criteria.

So if the prospect ticks any of the 'disqualification' list below, I will refer them on to someone else.

- if I feel they're just ticking a box for sales training and aren't willing to change
- if I don't like the way they talk about their sales team/staff on a human level
- if I feel I can't make a difference within the budget they have
- if I can't meet their timeline as I'm booked out
- if I feel it's a bad product and don't want to be associated with it
- if they haggle on price (these always end up being the hardest clients!)

These qualifying and disqualifying criteria are important, as they help to ensure you are spending less time on unsuitable leads. So if you haven't jotted yours down, and you're still reading, do go and make your list now!

So how do we ask these questions without being, well, rude (I see you cringing)?

Well, I'm here to help. Here are a few ways to bring up tricky qualifying questions. Try them out, tweak them, add your own fabulous flair and, of course, adjust them to fit your service or product.

Budget – this is a cheat sheet for bringing up budget

- Have you already had a look through our prices?- As we explore how best I can support you, it would be beneficial to touch upon budgetary considerations so I can customise a package that suits you.
- In order to recommend the right solutions for you it would be helpful to know what budget range you have in mind for this work, then we can explore solutions to fit.
- I would like to suggest a couple of solutions/packages for you but it would be good to know what kind of budget you are looking to invest in (this outcome).

Authority – cheat sheet for finding the decision maker(s)

- Who else, besides you, is involved in the decision making process for this?
- Could you help me understand how the decision making process works? Are there several people who decide or just one?
- Does anyone else need to come into this conversation who makes the call on going ahead?
- If there is anyone else who helps make the final decision? If so, could they come into our meeting too, or at least do they have any questions they would want me to answer when you discuss this with them?

Need – cheat sheet for finding out if they have a need

- What would you want our service/product to do for you/ your company?
- What outcomes are you looking for?
- What challenges or goals are you aiming for that you believe we could help you with?
- How are you currently handling (the problem you offer solve) and is there anything you think could be improved?
- In (your area of expertise), what are the main problems you need to address?
- If I could wave a magic wand and solve three things (around your area of expertise) what would they be?

Time – cheat sheet for finding out if the time is right

- In terms of implementing this, when were you looking at getting started?
- Are we looking at a particular timeframe for this solution/ purchase?
- Are there any external factors that might influence when we could start?
- Ideally, when would you like this service/product?

Those are a few suggestions, but you can adapt them to your own tone of voice, of course.

Key takeaways

- Know exactly what qualifies a great lead.
- Know exactly what disqualifies a lead for you.
- Understand that they may qualify later so keep in touch.
- Get comfy with asking the qualifying questions.

FREE EXTRA RESOURCES:

Having a checklist of qualifying criteria can be a useful prompt for sales calls and meetings, so you don't leave the chat thinking 'Argh I forgot to check about the other decision makers!' or similar. There is a downloadable free template you can use for both brain dumping and then prioritising your own personal criteria in the extra resources at https://www.nofluff.biz/spend-less-sell-more (or, you know the drill, scan the QR code).

Section 7.3
Not a Good Fit?

Ah, the inevitable question: What to do with the leads that aren't a perfect fit for your business? It's so hard to turn leads away, isn't it? You feel like you should cling on to every one. If you only have a few, and you have time to follow the one-page Follow-Up Framework that's coming your way, then go for it! However, if you are time-poor and have a good number of leads, it's important to spend less time on those who simply aren't going to buy.

It's like finding mismatched puzzle pieces in your inbox – they just don't quite click. But fear not, my friend, because we've got some solutions up our sleeves with which to turn this situation into an opportunity for growth and goodwill/ I hope this will enable you to walk away from bad-fit leads without feeling guilty.

First things first; let's start with a big old "Thank you!" Express your gratitude to these leads for showing interest and taking the time to reach out. Out of all the companies in all the world, they took time out to interact with YOU! How fantastic! A little appreciation goes a long way in building positive connections and maintaining your professional charm.

Instead of bidding them farewell with a sad sigh, consider these strategies to make the most of these not-so-perfect-fit leads:

1) Offer Alternatives: If your business isn't the perfect match for their needs, why not play the role of matchmaker? Suggest other businesses or professionals who might be a better fit. It's like being the Cupid of connections, spreading goodwill and building your network along the way.

2) Keep the Door Open: Even if the timing isn't quite right for them now, it doesn't mean it won't be in the future. Things change, budgets grow, and needs evolve. Stay in touch by inviting them to join your mailing list, keep a note of their details and schedule a gentle reminder to reconnect in the future. When the stars align, they will remember you and boomerang right back into your loving arms.

3) Share the Love: Remember, you're a source of wisdom and value, so spread it far and wide. Provide these leads with valuable resources, educational content, or free goodies that align with their needs. Sharing is caring, and by giving without expecting anything in return, you build goodwill and leave a lasting impression.

So, my empathetic entrepreneur, while these leads may not be the perfect fit for your business right now, remember that every interaction is an opportunity to leave a positive imprint. Approach each encounter with a mix of curiosity and professionalism, plus a sprinkle of kindness. But be pragmatic – if they're not a good-fit lead for you, move them on nicely.

Congratulations! You've cracked the code on identifying those hot prospects who are ready and able to jump on board with you. Now that you can swiftly separate the eager buyers from the casual observers, you're in for a treat – spending more time and energy focusing on the leads that truly matter.

By qualifying leads early on, you're doing yourself a massive favour. You're avoiding those moments when you realise that a lead simply can't afford what you are offering or isn't a good fit for your fantastic product or service. Moving your energy away from these leads is just as important as nurturing those who are a good match. It's a clever time-saving strategy that frees you up to shower attention on the blazing hot leads.

Remember, it's all about working smarter, not harder. Every minute you save by swiftly identifying unqualified leads is a minute you can spend nurturing those sizzling prospects who are primed and ready to become loyal customers. So, embrace the art of lead qualification with open arms, and find peace with saying farewell to the rest.

Now that you've got your qualification radar finely tuned, and you have your very own checklist of what is a fit, and what isn't, it's time to gear up for the next chapter: the magical world of leveraging existing leads. Get ready to discover how to transform those warm prospects into enthusiastic buyers who can't resist your offerings. It's a journey filled with excitement, creativity, and that special touch that sets you apart.

So, my resourceful lead qualifier, it's time to invest your time and energy where it truly counts – in nurturing those leads who are destined to become your biggest fans. Keep up the fantastic work, and let's dive into the realm of leveraging existing leads like the brilliant entrepreneur you are!

Key takeaways

- Ensure you know what your ideal clients look like.
- Target them with laser focus in your marketing.
- When leads come into your world, qualify them early on.
- Ensure you know exactly what your qualifying criteria are.
- Ensure you know what dis-qualifies a lead also.
- Decide how you will deal with dis-qualified leads.

Chapter 8
Progressing and Pipeline

You have probably heard of sales funnels, pipelines and all that jazz. You may already have them in place somehow. But let's get back to the basics here and just double check we are clear on what these are what the heck they are for.

A sales funnel and a sales pipeline both represent the stages of the customer journey, but they focus on different aspects of it. A sales funnel emphasises the buyer's journey from awareness to purchase. It visualises the overall process, highlighting conversion rates and drop-offs in general terms across all leads. We need to make sure we are attracting the right leads into the top of the funnel. Then we work on what needs to be done to move them from the top of the funnel, through each stage to the bottom.

For example, a lead might come into your funnel by interacting with your social media a few times. Then they might fill in an enquiry form. You might have a call to talk about options. Some emails may be exchanged about pricing and details. There may be other decision makers brought into an online meeting. The contract might then be sent, signed and finally paid (yay). Sold. They have travelled through your sales funnel from becoming aware of your offer, considering it (and you qualifying them as a good fit), negotiating detail (both sides) and then purchasing.

By contrast, a sales pipeline is a tool for sales teams to manage active deals. It gets more into the nitty-gritty. It shows where each deal is in the sales process and helps the team prioritise and track interactions with each lead. You'll usually see them in CRMs– each stage of the pipeline is called something different. They usually run from left to right with 'colder' leads on the left and 'closed' leads on the right. While a sales funnel is more customer-centric, a sales pipeline is salesperson-centric, aiding in deal progression and forecasting.

A sales pipeline is more granular. It looks at what stage that particular lead is in, diarises the touchpoints and estimates the value of that lead if they go on to purchase.

If I'm losing you here – WAIT!!! If talk of funnels and pipelines is putting you off, just think of the whole thing as checking that your lead is getting the attention, materials, information and love that they need at each stage in order to give you the best chance of helping them purchase from you. That's all it is. Your Follow-Up Framework is going to help you move them more easily through the stages.

So what are the stages..?

You can call them whatever you like. (It's your business, you do you!) For example, it could be as simple as a cold lead, warm lead, hot lead and superhot lead. I've even worked with a healer who now names her qualifying stages Seedling, Sprouting, Blooming, Ripe. You get the idea… you are taking a lead through stages to become a purchaser. Throughout the journey from discovering you to buying, they will become more and more "qualified" to purchase. And when you reach the end of this process, you either close the deal and win it, or close the deal because you didn't win it.

So while I'm all for fancy names and you enjoying your sales work, really what we are going to need is around four to six stages of qualifying a lead through to purchasing. Why am I saying four to six? Well, you may have certain additional stages you need to go through; for example, you may need to onboard and train them first if they are third parties selling your services or products.

A good example of this is the international education sector where, say, a language school would want to onboard education agents in other countries to recruit students for them. Their funnel and pipeline includes two processes; one is to find and onboard new agents, and the other is to encourage their onboarded agents to sell programs on their behalf – time and time again.

So here are a few examples you can use:

A simple qualifying process if you are selling directly to the consumer, or the end purchaser.

Cool
Warm
Hot
Superhot
Closed won
Closed lost

If you are using third party sellers you may need a longer pipeline if you only have one available, as one part is onboarding a new seller, and the next is for their order enquiries, it might instead be:

Cool
Warm

Hot
Onboarded
Enquiry in
Negotiation
Closed Won
Closed Lost

Whatever you label your pipeline stages, you should be clear on what criteria are needed to move onto the next stage. For example, what moves a lead from cold to warm? Is it a chance meeting at an event? A cheeky "like" on your socials? And what moves them from warm to hot? It should involve more indication that they're a potential buyer, so perhaps it is if they ask particular questions, or you have a meeting and qualify them as a good potential buyer. And from there, to get them to superhot what do they need? To say yes? To agree? To sign a contract? Decide what the criteria are.

And decide what a 'closed won' sale is. Is it as simple as they make payment? Or is it that they have signed a contract and have been trained to sell your services? Or is it more complicated?

As selling can be about having someone agree to represent you, or someone adopting your idea (e.g. it could be a boss agreeing to implement your masterplan; or a shop agreeing to stock your product), you need to define it clearly, as all roads lead to that point – but then perhaps you have other steps – such as – if they're selling your product in their store, do they then need help to train their their staff to know the selling points? Do they need marketing posters or materials? Do you somehow need to help their buyers with the purchase?

Get clear on the steps. It doesn't take long, but don't overcomplicate it; just try and keep your pipeline as simple as possible.

Why are we talking about pipelines and funnels when we are here to make our Follow-Up Framework? Well – you are going to find that leads can get stuck in one stage or another. Hopefully not; I mean, let's be optimistic! Hopefully they'll all seamlessly fly through each stage to purchase. But sometimes they will stall and hang around, taking it easy, in one stage. Now, if you find this happens at a particular stage pretty much all of the time, something is going wrong. But only by knowing the stages, and what you are doing at each to encourage progression, are you going to be able to pinpoint where they're all lounging around or – worse – disappearing off into the sunset.

With your trusty Follow-Up Framework in hand though, you are going to know exactly how to keep things going, just what to say or send, and how to do it on autopilot. Employ your Follow-Up Framework whenever a lead is still in that pipeline, and they have gone all quiet on you. And you can re-use it if they engage and then go quiet again! Just use different components.

The idea is, you haven't put all that effort into attracting the lead, getting them into your pipeline, chatting, and emailing for nothing. Let's move them on up!

Key takeaways

- Be clear on your pipeline stages.
- Be clear on exactly what each stage means.
- What boxes need to be ticked in order for a prospect to move from one to another?

Part III
Sell More – Making the Follow-Up Framework

Rightio then, this is where the pieces come together to create the masterpiece – your Follow-Up Framework. As we embark on this part of our book, we're setting our sights on one singular goal: crafting a follow-up plan that's not just effective, but converts leads into sales, particularly cold leads that have gone quiet on you.

Let's be clear; this isn't about crafting a framework riddled with complexity and intricacy. Instead, we're here to uncover the beauty of simplicity, to distill the essence of effective follow-up into a concise, actionable plan. Even if you don't have a CRM, automations or a massive team you can still use this Follow-Up Framework to make more sales. You just need the one-page Framework and a diary or calendar to put it to work.

So, let's get started!

Chapter 9
Make it Easy on Yourself

Want to make follow-up easier?

Always set the next step with the client while you're on the previous step.

Write that down. Stick it on your monitor. Live by it.

There are three scenarios here:

1) Set an agreed next step with the lead
2) Set a next-step expectation without their buy-in
3) Set a next step without even speaking to the lead

Why?

The reason for this is because, unless a lead has closed down or completely dropped off the face of the earth, they are still a lead. Especially if they're a qualified lead, even partially. Even if they've said no. And we know that leads say "no" multiple times before they say "yes".

Setting the next step avoids all the awkwardness – if you have a meeting in the diary that they agreed to, they're more likely to show up. If they know you're going to follow up in a few days (as you asked how long they needed to digest your information), they're likely to remember and take the call.

Here's an example from several years ago that I particularly like as it's simple! I was selling advertising space to educational institutions in the esteemed StudyTravel Magazine, which is targeted at education agent readers around the globe. Advertisers reach these agents, who send multiple students, year after year, to their educator partners. So each agent is worth a pretty penny to the educators, and in return, they take a commission.

Every so often I'd call the lovely chap in charge (let's call them Summer School, and him Bill). He would be polite and friendly, agree he wanted more international students, and tell me there was a marketing budget, but it wasn't going to be directed at our publication because our readers were agents, and they only wanted to market directly to students.

Fair enough, Bill. I appreciated him taking my call and chatting. He was a "qualified" lead in all but one criteria. He didn't need what I was selling. Damn!! Everything else was in place. He certainly had the potential to buy what I was selling if they changed tack. I couldn't include him in my deal pipeline as he wasn't fully qualified; in fact was definitely not fully qualified. So I just used the diary function in my CRM.

I diligently set the next few steps. These were to send him some copies of the magazine every few months, and then to call Bill back every year, around budget-setting time. Between times he would still receive my general emails so we'd keep him informed that way, too. But my own personal outreach call to him would be annual.

One call per year. Five minutes' work. And pleasant work, at that, for Bill is a lovely man.

In every call we had, I'd cheerily ask what was happening in his world and how the team were doing, and after he told me the same thing, I'd tell him I'd call him back in a year for an update again, and he'd say 'OK then, speak to you in a year'. I'd set the next step with him, pop it in my calendar, together with a couple of tasks to mail some copies to him, and leave him alone.

Five years later...

One time, I made the call and Bill had a different tone to his voice. He was clearly beaming away and told me that he had good news for me; they had decided to market to agents now and so our audience was finally relevant! We laughed – he knew I'd been waiting five years for this. We discussed his options, and he bought some advertising space, and some space at our conferences too. And Summer School has been a great client ever since.

The point is that the next step was set with him; he knew I'd call him regularly and was happy to take that call. The follow-up step wasn't within a week or a month, it was at the right pace for this particular lead given his qualifying status. The touchpoints between the annual call were the regular emails (no cost or effort from me) and the mailing of the materials twice (low cost and only the effort of a including handwritten note with it). Plus, he was always fun to chat to, and that helps!

Tenacity and persistence, without pressure.

He knew I'd call. He was expecting it. And not at all resistant to it.

Set the next step. This is your new mantra.

Even if you have gone through your Follow-Up Framework, and reached the end, diarise the next step. It might be a quick 'checking-in' type of email (though don't say "checking in", as it makes people squirm); or it might be a quick call. For the sake of a few seconds' work, there is always a next step.

Let's consider a few examples.

1) Set an agreed next step with the lead

   That next step is ideally made together with the lead. You pop it in the diary and invite them. You embrace it as a way to demonstrate reliability and trustworthiness. They know the next step so it's much more likely to go ahead. It is a fantastic buying signal. At the very least, it means they are flirting with the idea of hearing you out!

2) Set a next step expectation without buy-in

   Even if your lead hasn't set the next step with you – go ahead and set it anyway. You can either let them know, or just plan it.

   For example you can try the "reverse call to action" which is when you tell them what is going to happen next, and they don't necessarily need to do anything, take any action, or remember or diarise it.

   It can be as simple as: "I'll give you a call back on Friday morning."

   They know it's happening, but you don't necessarily need their agreement or buy-in. Obviously, having their agreement would be brilliant – but if they are low commitment, you're just going to have to set that next step and do it anyway.

3) Set a next step without even speaking to the lead

   Even if you haven't spoken to them, don't forget to set the next step. This is the basis of the Follow-Up Framework! Don't worry, we will walk through how to do it. But Set The Next Step is the mantra. You are going to follow up. You will diarise it. You will know what you're going to say. You will know which method to use. You're going to love it!

It is truckloads easier to follow up when you have already laid the groundwork.

So let's start focusing on making the Framework!

Key takeaways

- Always set the next step
- Always diarise the next step

FREE EXTRA RESOURCES:

Sometimes we need a visual reminder! Head to the extra resources online to grab a mini poster to stick near your monitor to remind you to set the next step! You can scan the QR code or type this link in to get it:
https://www.nofluff.biz/spend-less-sell-more

Chapter 10
When

Section 10.1
Why "When" is Important

I can feel your excitement – and nervousness – about jumping right into creating that timetable on your Follow-Up Framework, but before we do, we need to distinguish between two lead superheroes when it comes to that crucial first follow-up.

Behold, our dynamic duo: Inbound and Outbound leads. Now, don't worry, this won't be a lengthy blah-de-blah. In fact, it's a swift but important explanation that will affect the "when" of your follow-up. So strap in and get ready to unravel the secrets of these lead legends!

Inbound lead: a prospective buyer who finds you for themselves (so they have heard of and interacted with your business in some way before).

Outbound lead: a prospective buyer that you reach out to in the first instance (who may not have heard of your business ever before).

INBOUND leads – the first response

"I feel the need, the need for speed"

– Maverick, from ***Top Gun***

When it comes to inbound leads, whether they come through web forms, phone calls, texts, or good old face-to-face encounters, speed is the name of the game. We're talking Usain Bolt-level speed here! In fact, did you know that a staggering 78% of leads buy from the first to respond? It's a race against time, and being the fastest responder gives you a competitive edge.

So, how fast should you be (I see you sweating already)? Well, if it's humanly possible, aim to respond within five minutes. Yes, you read that right – five minutes! Why the need for speed, you ask? Well, studies have consistently shown that responding within this golden timeframe can increase your conversion rate by a whopping eight times. And because you want to spend less on leads but sell more, capitalising on this advantage is essential.

Think about it – in today's fast-paced world, nobody likes to wait. We're all in a hurry, with short attention spans and the need for instant gratification. We get fidgety if a website takes a few seconds to load. So, imagine the impact of making a potential customer wait for your response. It's like throwing a wet blanket on their enthusiasm and risking them moving on to your competitors. This is especially the case for larger purchases and personal investment. If I'm excited about booking onto a program, for example, and I send an enquiry, I want you to get in touch straight away and get excited with me! If you offer to help me through the process, if you seem like you really care about me and my decision, and we are both optimistic and happy, I am much more likely to make the purchase. If, however, you sound a bit bored, I'm likely to lose my enthusiasm. After all, you probably have hundreds of enquiries and buyers purchase the same thing all the time. For you, it's not that exciting. But, and I'll say it again – it's not about YOU.

Deep down, you already know this. You understand the impatience and the desire for immediate results. And let's face it, you don't want to miss out on opportunities by being sluggish in your response time. That's why it's time to channel your inner Maverick (sans the jet fighter) and embrace the need for speed in your follow-up process.

Now, I get it – responding within five minutes may not always be feasible, especially if you're dealing with a high volume of leads, working in a different time zone to your customer, or have a small team. But that doesn't mean you can't strive for efficiency. Implement systems and tools that allow you to respond as quickly as possible, automate certain processes, and prioritise your leads based on their potential value.

Remember, being lightning-fast in your response not only increases your chances of closing the deal but also showcases your professionalism and dedication to customer service. It sets you apart from the competition and leaves a lasting impression on your leads (even if they're not ready to buy yet).

So, follow-up number 1 is your response to the initial inbound enquiry. Now let's talk about an initial contact with a lead that you have generated yourself with your outreach.

OUTBOUND leads

If you're feeling brave, and being proactive, you will also be reaching out to potential buyers. In fact, I'd urge you to. I believe it is an integral part of the sales function to go and "hunt" for leads, collaborators and introducers.

This might mean that you head to an exciting event where you'll be able to meet potential buyers, or re-sellers, like an exhibition or trade show.

Often it is a mass email out to your audience in the hope some will open the message and some will even respond. It may be more personalised than that (I hope) and you're sending individual emails to well-researched matches that fit your ideal client avatar sketch.

Or it might be that you're hitting the phones and calling through some prospective leads (which I celebrate, by the way! You are my kind of person!)

In these outbound cases, when you connect with the lead (so that means you meet them, you chat with them or they respond to your beautifully crafted email), you'll be following up on a much more personalised level, as you will have carried out some discovery during that time and can better tailor your response. When you're chatting to someone and find out their needs, pain points, hopes, dreams and family dog's name, you can much more effectively tailor your offer to all of that – as well as building a fabulous rapport. So the follow-up after this chat changes a little depending on what was said, and what next step you agreed.

You did agree a next step, didn't you?

Tip:

In every sales interaction – set the next step. Even when you get a "we'll get back to you if we're interested" reply. It is your job to follow up, and you're not about to lose control of this process and sit there at your desk waiting like a lost puppy for their response to your email. Stretch yourself a little here and let them know, nicely, what will happen next.

You can aim to fix the next meeting and send a calendar invitation.

You can let them know that you'll call back on a certain day to check progress.
You can book in a demo or tour with a colleague.
You can offer to visit them on a particular day.
Whatever it may be – make sure they are expecting the next step (unless they have definitively said "no don't bother me again").

The point of setting the next step is to help you with the Follow-Up Framework. If you've set the next meeting or call, you're good to go! Make sure it's in the diary. If, however, they don't show up or answer, revert to the Framework.

Rule 1: If you fix a date and time between you, that's when your next contact is.

Rule 2: If you don't, or one of you isn't aware of the next touchpoint, you follow the Framework.

Right, so now we know the difference between an inbound and outbound lead, and we've covered that first response, we are going to tackle the "when" head on.

When to get back to a lead is important, you've sent your blurb or explained it all, then what?

When should you pop up again and check if they have any questions or if they received your email? Or (ahem) ask if they want to buy? And what if you don't get a response? Do you just leave it be?

Ah, the art of the gentle nudge. We want to strike the right balance between staying on their radar and avoiding that feeling of being overly pushy. After all, nobody wants to feel sick about follow-up, whether it is you or the lead!

So, how can we do it without feeling icky? How can we do it without making the lead feel icky? How can we do it so we stay front-of-mind, and they feel valued. Let's dive in!

Timing is key. You want to find that sweet spot where you're proactive without being intrusive.

I'll give you an example.

A client of mine (let's call him Dave) went to a trade show where they had speed-date type meetings with potential resellers, meaning big bucks if even just one came on board. A TON of great leads! Truly a great way to start that relationship in person. And Dave had paid a chunky amount to attend this, so he really wanted to make this work.

When we looked at his follow-up Dave usually sent them the information they'd discussed within a week.

He was pretty chuffed at this. After all, he had had around 45 meetings over one weekend; that was a lot to get through and personalise! Plus he was exhausted. Back-to-back meetings and social events over two days had been quite a marathon. Nothing he couldn't handle, of course; he was a sociable and extroverted type. But, it had been hard going, and he could barely smile at his family once he got home. Moreover, then he had to catch up on the day job the next day.

Now, that all may well be true, but let's look at the reseller's journey, let's call our reseller Oscar. He was super friendly, well connected, handsome and charming! He was passionate about his sector and loved these events. Oscar also had back-to-back meetings over two days. He had flown into the UK from Spain for this event the day before and still had staff pinging him messages throughout.

While Oscar was quite happy and energised for the whole event, he had businesses pitching at him every 30 minutes, all day, and in the evenings for two days straight. He had to decide who to trust, who he liked, and who had the goodies he needed, at the right price for his clients. But mostly, the point of the meetings was to establish a relationship. This was the best way to see the whites of each other's eyes, after all, Oscar would be trusting the provider with his reputation and clients' wellbeing, if he didn't trust and like the provider, they were unlikely to work together.

After the event Oscar was invited to visit various providers' offices and he was scooted off and wined and dined further. After he was sure he couldn't smile any more he headed to the airport to fly home. Several hours later he is back "en casa" and putting his feet up, ready to slay the next working day, or perhaps even catching up with emails until late so his inbox isn't a scary place to visit the next morning.

So what does Oscar want? An email with pdfs a week later? Maybe. But also, consider this; his meeting with Dave was on the Saturday at 9am.Before that even happened, Oscar had met a gaggle of eager suppliers in the networking events the night before. He had been accosted in the coffee queue by a supplier who wanted a meeting but Oscar's schedule was full. He then made it to Dave's table for the first official appointment of the day at 9am.

By the time Oscar has Dave's follow-up email in his inbox he has been through a LOT. Not only all the other meetings at the workshop, but familiarisation visits to providers' premises, fielding calls from the office, a flight home, family time, a week of office meetings and catching up on the day job.Oscar is a busy guy! Dave has always thought that waiting a week for the follow-up email to go is considerate. And I get the point. However, by the time Dave's email lands in Oscar's inbox, Oscar has met, in person, around 60 competing suppliers. Dave needs to stand out. He needs to follow up sooner, but also in a way that is sympathetic to what is happening in Oscar's life at that point. Not necessarily a long email with his entire brochure and 10 paragraphs of text.

But one week later…? On top of the 60 or so competing suppliers Dave is competing with, after one week back in the office Oscar has been dealing with the day job, having meetings with his team, met his web developer, been out for dinners with friends, had a migraine, got stressed with a client, made and received plenty of phone calls, had around 300 emails. Frankly, he has gone off the boil on everything Dave talked about in those 30 minutes a week ago.

That was then. However… Ta -da! NOW, Dave has his Follow-Up Framework, so he is a sales superhero. Now what happens in these meetings goes a little like this…

First of all, Dave pre-qualifies every meeting he makes. He calls Oscar (and the other suppliers) weeks before the event even starts, so they have all the pdfs and brochures that they could need and have established that there is a possible match between them.

By the time the meeting comes around, rapport has already partly been established. They have their thirty minute chat with more knowledge about each others needs so they could get into the nitty gritty.

Dave sets up the next step in the meeting itself. Dave and Oscar have a date in the diary for one week's time to go into more detail and lay out some training for Oscar's team. So, after their 9am meeting at the event, Dave sends a follow-up email, brief, focused, and immediately after the meeting. Dave ensures it is a friendly extension of their meeting. He refers to some of the chit-chat they had and uses his authentic 'tone of voice'. It demonstrates that he values Oscar's business and time. He shows that he cares about Oscar's business and that he follows up swiftly (which is important if he is to look after Oscar's clients in a timely fashion). The day before the follow-up meeting is scheduled, Dave sends a WhatsApp to Oscar with the selfie they took at the event, and says he's looking forward to their meeting the next day.

By finding the right balance and approaching follow-up with authenticity and value, you can maintain a positive connection with leads without feeling sleazy or overwhelming them.

Don't worry, I've got you. I'm going to softly stretch your comfort zone while at the same time ensuring you get the follow up done. This One Page Follow-Up Framework is YOURS, not mine. There's no point making a Framework if you're not going to stick to it, but I will advise you, and it's coming from decades of experience in multiple teams.

So before we start I'm going to give you some guidance.

One piece of advice I'd like to stick. And that is:

You are going to need to follow up more than you already are.

I'm going to urge you to go with the flow of the guidelines, and trust the process. You are making your own, personalised Follow-Up Map, a guide on converting more leads into sales. I will not be standing over your shoulder, arms crossed, head cocked to the side, tutting away, making sure you stick to it, people pay me for that kind of work ;-)

"If it scares you, it might be a good thing to try."

– Seth Godin

Section 10.2
Plotting the When

Follow up number	When?	How?	Value Add?	Call to Action?
Follow-up 1 Enquiry IN/ Outbound connection				
Follow-up 2				
Follow-up 3				
Follow-up 4				
Follow-up 5				
Follow-up 6				
Follow-up 7				
Follow-up 8				

Right then! Grab your Follow-Up Map template, make one, or go and download the free one here: https://www.nofluff.biz/spend-less-sell-more

Then go down the first column marked 'when'.

Follow-up 1: Write down how long you will leave it before replying to an inbound lead or sending your info after an outbound reach-out.

I would recommend doing so within five minutes. If you have to gather complex pieces of information this can be longer, of course, but within the hour if at all possible.

Did they reply? Get back to them and schedule Follow-up 2 from that point.

Follow-up 2: Now, how long will you leave it before contacting them again? I would recommend between half a day and 2 days. Don't forget, you're not necessarily expecting them to have made a decision in this time; it's a gentle nurture, a nudge and little show of attention to make sure they know you value their business. So be brave and bring this forward. Quite often, when I ask when they follow up in a training session, I'm given the answer of "one week later". Now I want you to think about the last time you considered buying something, after one week did you still feel enthused about it? Had you calmed down a little? Were you, by this point, comparing it to other options? Had the "other options" been in touch and also sounded good? And do you want your leads to feel like this too? Do you want them to lose their excitement and enthusiasm? Do you want to leave a big gap for competitors to call them and fire them up again?

Did they reply? Get back to them and schedule Follow-up 3 from that point.

Follow-up 3: Now. They've not replied to the last follow. Don't forget, most of the people I train used to give up here! This is going to sort the wheat from the chaff. (Gosh, one of my mum's sayings has crept in – let's keep it – she'll be pleased). You aren't going to give up at this point. Remember you have spent time and money on getting this lead in. You may even have at least partially qualified this lead, so we need to crack on.

For follow-up 3, I would recommend waiting a maximum of two days after the last point of contact. Remember, this is YOUR Follow-up Framework. You have drawn out your ideal client avatar. You know that you are probably holding yourself back from pursuing the sale because your own mindset monkeys are having a party up in your head. Don't let them distract you – we are going to follow-up in ways that are not sleazy, pushy, or time-wasting. Instead, we are going to make your leads feel valued, listened to, interested and enthused. Why would you deny them that? Plot Follow-up 3 into your Framework.

Did they reply? Get back to them and schedule Follow-up 4 from that point.

Follow-up 4: I know, it's getting tricky now and you're already thinking you should leave it now. I promise you, not all of your leads have given up on YOU at this point. They're still thinking it over. Still deciding. Maybe they're just distracted and busy. But you can either remind them of your fabulousness, or you can let it slide. Do you want to let it slide? Are you ready to give up on your business? Is it worth a few minutes of your time to do the next follow-up? Right, then plot Follow-up 4. I would, again, recommend, around another two to three days for this one.

If you've followed my guidelines, so far we are between four and a half and eight days. Eight days between that first point of contact and follow-up 4 is actually quite a long time. If this were you, waiting for a text from a new love interest, you'd be pretty annoyed at this timeframe, wouldn't you?

Did they reply? Get back to them and schedule Follow-up 5 from that point.

Follow-up 5: If you aren't a sales professional by trade and you're not used to following up three times, let alone five, you are likely to be squirming, wondering if you can skip to the next part and just see how three or four follow-ups work before you venture onto the rest of this column? I see you. I know. But I promise, your lead is not going to be thinking as much about this as you are. You are making this bigger in your head than it needs to be. When we finish your beautiful Framework, you'll feel better. So please just carry on and plot follow-up 5. I'm going to recommend waiting around three days here.

Follow-up 6: Have you ever followed up six times? You're going to, now you know better! Just jot down in this section of the column how long is a good amount of time to leave it. Personally, I'd go for around three days again but you may want to leave it five days if that is more comfortable. It has to be manageable. But it also has to be done, so pop your number in here.

Follow-up 7: Let's keep going. We may as well start with good intentions! How long before you send them another note or give them a quick call? I'd go for around 2 days. Remember, they will not be obsessing about this nearly as much as you will be. And also remember, you are not selling at each of these follow-ups. You're just helping them, keeping them engaged and staying front of mind.

Follow-up 8: This is the last follow-up I'm going to ask you to note down – this can be a week or two after Follow-up 7.

What happens if Follow-up 8 fails to engage them? Don't worry, I've got you. We're going to cover that later on. For now, just go through the process of filling in this Framework with me.

So now we have a column full of good intentions. These should be do-able, though they should stretch your comfort zone. They should be spaced well so that the lead doesn't lose interest, or go with a competitor, but wide enough that they end up blocking you. Having said that, if they block you, they probably weren't your ideal client anyway.

At the moment you may be looking back at the numbers in the columns and worrying they are too close. Stop right there. We will not make this all about the "when". We will make it all about the "Value Add". Your persistence will work in your favour. It won't feel to the lead like you're interrupting, being pushy and so on. Trust the process. And with that, let's move on to "How".

Key takeaways

- Decide how much time between each touchpoint you will leave
- Plot the 'When' column
- Stretch yourself!

Chapter 11
How

By incorporating a variety of outreach methods into your follow-up strategy, you create a well-rounded approach that resonates with different types of buyer. Avoid relying solely on one method (be honest... you mainly use email, right?) Instead, embrace diversity to engage leads on multiple levels. Each interaction brings you one step closer to building meaningful rapport and unlocking new opportunities for sales.

This is already a big step. However, you may be wondering how to refine these channels for your target audience. I'd still recommend mixing up your channels and never relying on just one (unless they are responding – then you've hit gold. Keep going on that channel until they go quiet!) However, here are some tips on each age group. [11:1]

Section 11.1 Considering Generations

Gen Z (Born 1997-2012)

Their Go-To Channels

Instagram messages, WhatsApp, and instant messaging such as SnapChat.

Their preferred hangout?

- Instagram: Over 75% pop in daily.
- WhatsApp: 60% see it as their digital chatroom.
- Phone Calls: For a select 25%, old-school is still cool.

Where do they engage the most?

- Instagram: High – especially if it's visually catchy.
- WhatsApp: Prompt and pretty active.
- Email and Phone: A tad quieter.

Type of content?

Brevity is your friend, visuals are allies, and staying updated is key.

Gen Z, or "Zoomers", have this not-so-secret confession: phone calls? Not their thing. A solid 60% would rather skip making that call to book a dentist appointment. They'd love for someone else to do the dialling or just whip out an app or shoot off a text.

Almost 80% slide into those DMs, whether to sing praises, drop some constructive "tea", or just shoot off a query. They are not shy if you're on their turf. But mass emails? That's a no-no. They like one-to-one communication and expect to feel one-of-a-kind. So be careful that any automations or templates you use are pretending to be individually crafted. If they aren't, you'll be sniffed out and cast as a fraud. They aren't against newsletters and the like, but they want to feel understood. The message needs to be "Hey, I see YOU."

Plot twist! Their love for one-to-one can really work in your favour at trade shows and events. A good 40% of our Zoomer buyers treasure face-to-face catch-ups.

Millennials (Born 1981-1996)

Their Go-To Channels:

Email (yep, they're keeping it alive!), WhatsApp, and a dose of Instagram.

Their preferred hangout:

- Email: 85% are still dedicated to the inbox hustle.
- WhatsApp: 70% lounge here for chit-chats.
- Instagram: 65% make regular appearances.

Where do they engage the most?

- Email: Solid, especially with a touch of personal flair.
- WhatsApp: Robust and responsive.
- Phone Calls: A bit of a mixed bag.

Type of content?

Infuse your personality into your text; they want to know you're human, so add value and treat them as individuals.

Millennials? They love SMS. "75% of Millennials would rather lose the ability to talk versus text," according to OpenMarket. And even if you're rolling your eyes at this, we have to go where the leads are.

Why? Texts let them play by their own rules. According to the Conversational Advertising report by MobileSquared around 90% open texts within 3 minutes. They can peek at messages, mull them over while eating their smashed avocado toast, and reply when they're ready. Phone calls, with their "answer now" vibes? A tad too pushy. However, if they think it's an official call, they'll often answer, so it shouldn't be ruled out of your "how" column.

Gen X (Born 1965-1980)

Their Go-To Channels: Emails (timelessly chic), trusty Phone Calls, and a hint of WhatsApp.

Their Preferred Hangout:

- Email: 34% consider it their digital home base.
- Phone Calls: The favoured way to connect for many.
- WhatsApp: A comfortable 50% have hopped on.

Where do they engage the most?

- Email: Consistently strong.
- Phone Calls: Still a winner.
- WhatsApp: Respectable, but with room for growth.

Type of Content?

Blend the timeless with the modern, and be direct.

Gen X finds itself sitting on both sides of the technology fence. Having grown up in a blend of old school and digital they are not to be underestimated. For them, a good old email and a straight-up phone call still win, rocking over a 50% preference rate for both. And while they aren't outraged at the use of SMS marketing like their Boomer counterparts, they're not quite as text-happy as the millennial crowd.

Baby Boomers (Born 1946-1964)

Their Go-To Channels: Phone Calls and the ever-reliable Email.

Where do they hang out?

- Phone Calls: The first pick for over 80%.
- Email: 70% are regular checkers.
- WhatsApp: A curious 30% peek in.

Where do they engage the most?

- Phone Calls: Exceptionally responsive.
- Email: Steady and dependable.
- WhatsApp: A gentle nudge might be needed.

Type of content?

Prioritise trust, clarity, and simplicity.

Just as millennials do a double-take at unexpected calls, Baby Boomers often give the side-eye to random text pings.

Boomers are all about keeping it straightforward. Nothing beats a good face-to-face chat for them. But when that's not on the cards, a good old-fashioned phone call will do. That said, with 2020 and lockdowns they learned to pivot, and they warmed up to digital channels such as SMS, FaceTime and WhatsApp.

Also, it's worth noting that their trust in text-based communication is low – having heard many of the scams around, they are nervous. They would rather see the whites of your eyes.

Section 11.2
Types of 'How'

We are so lucky that in today's world we can get in touch with our leads in such a wide variety of ways. But we all favour one method over another. And for many, that is still email. Good old email! We love it! However, email is a noisy place. We get so many of them each day that our inboxes bulge. So we should consider different touchpoints when trying to engage our chilly leads.

Here are some different touchpoints and methods for following up with leads:

1) Phone Call: A personal phone call can be a direct and effective way to connect with a lead, answer their questions, and build rapport. It is my favourite method. It is genius for getting immediate responses, gauging that response, asking questions more informally, and establishing yourself as a flesh-and-bones human rather than a fairly anonymous email. Resistance to making sales calls is lethal, especially in a B2B sales role. Be mindful that it might be your hang-up, rather than your lead's, as the statistics say that calls are welcomed. What statistics? Here you go:

   69% of buyers accepted a call from new salespeople in the past 12 months according to a comprehensive Rain Group study[11:2]. So, they are happy to take your call; you just need to make it! And before you say it doesn't work with the big cheeses, the same study showed that 57% of C-level buyers prefer salespeople to call them.

2) Email: Sending personalised emails is a common way to follow-up with leads. THE most common, in fact, so you won't

be alone in that inbox, your competitors will be there too, plus a ton of other emails that your lead has to deal with. However, it is an efficient way of providing additional information, especially anything data-led, and for sharing relevant content. The main reason emails don't convert is that there often hasn't been enough discovery done on the lead.

In fact, 59% of buyers think the sales emails they receive are irrelevant, according to a **Direct Marketing Association study[11:3]. A Salesforce survey[11:4]** found that more than 50% of customers will find someone else – even when they're looking for a provider – if they don't receive personalised emails. So, while I advocate saving time by using templates, please use them as a baseline for your messages. Personalisation is key. And if you can't personalise them – call instead!

In general, 33% of recipients open an email because of its subject line alone [11:5] . And including the recipient's first name in the subject line can boost open rates by 29.3%. Try it out yourself.

3) Social Media: Engaging with leads on social media platforms like Instagram,LinkedIn, Twitter, or Facebook can help build relationships either with comments and interactions or "in the DMs" – direct messages – particularly the business platforms such as LinkedIn. They will check you out! 82% of buyers look up providers on LinkedIn before they respond to their outreach efforts, according to The Rain Group survey [11:6] so you need to make sure your own content is helpful and relevant.

   By being more active on the social media of your leads you build trust and rapport. I am not a big fan of cold, sleazy, DMs. Personally, I see it as part of the trust-building process and getting to know my potential clients. I connect with them, like some of their posts, comment on them, share them and only after I've been doing that a while would I send a direct message. And it wouldn't be salesy – it would be a simple question or comment on something they've posted about or shared.

I would recommend you up your LinkedIn game by following advice from some of the leaders in this field such as Helen Tudor or Daniel Disney.

4) Text or WhatsApp Message: A quick, informal text message can be a friendly touchpoint enabling you to check in with leads and provide updates. In fact they have the best open rate of all channels, not surprisingly, as they are immediately delivered to the pocket of the lead. However, I believe it is best used after the initial contact has already been made and be mindful of your Ideal Client Avatar. My teens wouldn't think twice about engaging over text. (They only check emails when they are expecting something and won't take a phone call). My German aunt, however, would feel a WhatsApp used too early was intrusive and would prefer an email or a phone call.

   Texting or WhatsApping someone after having made contact leads to a 112.6% higher lead-to-engagement conversion. This is not least because of their open rates. Text messages have an open rate of 98%. WhatsApp's open rate is 99%, and it has a reply rate of 40%. So, don't forget to ask for their mobile/ WhatsApp! [11:7]

5) Video Message: Sending a personalised video message can create a more memorable and engaging follow-up experience. This could be using WhatsApp or by embedding a video into your email using something like Bonjoro, Vidyard or Loom .

Teams that use video enjoy a 16% bump in open rates and a remarkable 26% increase in replies [11:8].

6) Webinar or Workshop Invitation: invite leads to participate in a live webinar or online workshop to showcase your expertise and offer value. This isn't a one-to-one interaction, but it can help you to see if they are still engaged in your offer and give you good follow-up fodder for after the event.

7). Direct Mail: Send physical materials, such as postcards or brochures, to stand out and leave a tangible impression. Most mail these days is very bland so by sending something more exciting, you're going to stand out. However, it is a more costly option.

8) Referral: It might be you have a mutual connection who can facilitate a meeting – this is harder to navigate, but don't rule it out if the lead is a potential biggie! 92% of buyers trust referrals from people they know [11:9]. However, most people don't ask to be introduced. Find a mutual connection and ask them to refer you or have a virtual meeting or an in-person coffee together.

9) In Person: knocking on doors was the way they used to do it; while it isn't always possible, it can work wonders, particularly in the business-to-business world. Having said that, it's worth messaging ahead of time to say you'll be dropping in. It's also quite time-consuming, but worth including in our list.

Section 11.3
Plotting the How

Now we have looked into the different methods of communication, all those touchpoint options you have, just choose one for each of your Follow-ups in the Framework.

Sometimes you may need two – which might be if you have a call scheduled in, but there's no answer, in which case you might leave a voice note instead and say you'll drop them an email/WhatsApp/DM and to look out for it; and then send them whatever it is you promised.

Go ahead and fill out the "How" part of your Follow-Up Framework so we can move on to the exciting Value Add section! You're going to love this!

Key takeaways

- Mix up your touchpoints.
- Adjust the methods to suit the ideal client avatars.
- Don't stick to just one (email, I'm looking at you).
- Plot the "How" column.

Chapter 12
Value Add

In the world of sales and marketing, adding value at every interaction is the secret formula that turns ordinary follow-ups into extraordinary opportunities. Gone are the days of pushy sales tactics and aggressive persuasion. Ditch the fake urgency and "only two left" pitches, as nobody believes them anyway. Instead, we can embrace a new approach – one that revolves around genuine care, authentic connections, and empowering our leads to make informed decisions on their terms.

When we add value into our follow-ups, we create an authentic connection with our leads. They see us as trusted advisors, guiding them on their journey to success, rather than salespeople trying to meet targets. By providing valuable content and insights, we build relationships that go beyond a transactional exchange. And what does that mean? Not only buyers, but raving fans! Referrals! Free word of mouth marketing! Spending less!

Thou shalt not say "Did you get my email?" over and over again

At the core of value-driven follow-ups is the respect we have for our leads' time. We understand that their lives are busy, and bombarding them with generic sales pitches, or the same email several times with a "did you get my email" line added is not the way to go.

With every follow-up, we'll deliver value that leaves a lasting impression. We'll go beyond the sale, focusing on building relationships that endure. We'll be the ones who make their lives better, who make them smile, and who help them achieve their goals.

Section 12.1
How to Add Value

That's all very well, I hear you say, but how? What do we actually SAY? Well, that very much depends on your ideal client avatar, which is why we worked on this earlier in the book. Get back into their shoes, imagine you are that person, in their office/café/home. What would they value, right now? It does not have to be about your specific product or service. It does not even have to be something you have produced (though it is good practice to credit your source).

Here are some examples I have used:

- For my frazzled summer school operator in July: a link to five suggestions for de-stressing in two minutes (not my content - YouTube was my friend).
- For my sales director client who was hiring a new team member: a link to an article on great sales recruitment questions (this was follow-up 4). And a few days later, follow-up 5 was a video comedy sketch about terrible interviewees. Again, not even my own content. She sent me a voice note to thank me and we fixed a date to book coaching for when her newbie started.

- For the CEO of a company I was trying to land: an excerpt and link to market analysis of his sector was follow-up number 3. I'm still going on this one…!
- For a connection whose event I wanted to speak at but hadn't heard back from: follow-up number 4 was a direct message on LinkedIn saying that I noticed that they'd changed venues. (The 'I noticed that…' technique works well). I am speaking there every year now.
- For my tightly budgeted prospect new to sales: follow-up number 2 was a past recording of a masterclass I had delivered on closing techniques. They are yet to buy from me, but are a big fan, regardless.
- For a last-ditch outreach to a fun prospect that had ghosted me, follow-up 9 was a meme of Bridget Jones eating ice cream on her own saying 'All by myself' and asking him to get in touch before I resorted to surrounding myself with cats. He sent me a gif on WhatsApp of an old lady surrounded by cats. For follow-up 10, I called him, and he has now booked.
- For an education advisor who needed some fresh places to find leads: follow-up 2 was my *20 Places to Find More Students* eBook. As yet she hasn't purchased from me, but has referred two connections of hers who are now clients of mine.
- For a previous client I wanted to renew, but who had gone quiet, a handwritten postcard at follow-up 5. He took a photo of it and posted it on his socials, and I ended up with a new lead who got in touch after seeing it. He is now a dear client.

- For a hesitant lead: follow-up 3 was a case study of a former client in a similar situation, together with their testimonial quote of the results they had after working with me. The lead reached out to this former client to check up on me, and then booked.

So you see that you do not have to spend hours creating new things to entice your leads to respond and then purchase from you. You just need to use your emotional intelligence to tap into what they need right now. And as each ideal client avatar is similar, you can make a list of Value Adds. Then pop them into conversation or an email or DM.

Start a folder.

If you have more than one ideal client avatar, start one for each. Call that folder 'Value Add'. Start collecting things in these folders that your ideal clients might like.

What, though?! OK calm down, I'm going to give you some suggestions.

1) Video Magic: Do you have any videos you can send? Maybe a tour of your facility; some past client video testimonials; scenes of you delivering the service/making the product. Videos are engaging. You can either link to them with a short description or embed the video, if it's small.

2) Video of YOU magic!

   Picture this: you pop into their inbox with a delightful personalised video message that says, "Hello [Lead's Name]!" Ideally the thumbnail in the video will say their name to encourage them to open it. Share some nifty tips or show off a neat demo. Keep it fairly short though!

3) Thoughtful Emails with a Twist:

   No more snooze-worthy "checking in" emails. Spice things up with valuable content such as blog posts, eBooks, or snazzy industry reports relevant to their exact needs.

4) Thrilling Tales of Success:

   Stories sell well. Pull out the big guns with captivating case studies. Showcasing real-life success stories will have them thinking, "Wow, they really get us!" or "If they can do it, so can I!" They need 'social proof' in order to trust you.

5) VIP Access to Exclusive Webinars:

   Roll out the virtual red carpet and invite them to VIP-only webinars. Share insider insights, industry trends, and expert know-how. They'll be starstruck by your knowledge and support.

6) Fun-Filled Interactive Quizzes:

   Turn learning into a game with interactive quizzes or assessments. Help them discover their pain points, and then shower them with personalised solutions. There are several well established quizzes out there, for example TryInteract and ScoreApp.

7) Snails sometimes win:

   In a world of digital everything, your personal touch will stand out from the crowd. A postcard, a handwritten note, a book with a sticky note on it saying why you thought they'd enjoy it. Snail mail may take a bit longer but if that lead is worth the investment in postage and time – go for it. Nobody else will be doing it so you'll have the advantage.

8) Exclusive Offers:

   While I'm not a big fan of discounting – adding value can literally mean adding value: offering an extra "thing" free or adding an extra incentive. This could be a discount if profit margins allow, but be wary, as, if you discount all the time, you can never go back to full price.

9) Social Media Showdown:

   Engage, engage, engage! Bring on the social media charm with likes, comments, and shares. Let them know you're there for them. Support their efforts. Read their posts and blogs. Share them with your network.

10) Articles and pieces of interest:

   Gather the latest news and stats about your markets and share the links. For example, it might be a market report on their sector, or government changes that will affect them. Use credible sources and ask them what their thoughts are, to encourage engagement.

11) Virtual and-In Person Events:

   Invite them to an event you are hosting, or ask if they're attending an event you'll be going to. See if you can meet there, or ask what they're looking forward to.

12) Make them laugh:

   You need to be a little brave and confident for this one, but I'm a big fan, as all my clients have a good sense of humour. Play it pretty safe, but appeal to their humour with a meme, gif, video clip or similar.

It's time for a virtual extravaganza! Roll out the red carpet for online events, workshops, and meetups. It's networking heaven with a dash of valuable takeaways.

For some of these you may need to get creative. But for many of them you can use other peoples' content so don't let fear of creating fabulous Value Add pieces stop you in your Follow-Up Framework tracks. There is no need!

Section 12.2
Plotting the Value Add

Now you have some Value Add pieces, go ahead and plot them in your Framework template. The first follow-up is always going to be "whatever they asked for" with a few suggestions, depending on the enquiry or conversation. But after that, start with what you think is the strongest piece of value, then the next strongest and so on.

Some follow-ups are on the phone or via voice note or video, so remember to adjust your value add to the channel you're using. For example, 'I noticed that…' is easily used in a voice note or video. But a download is easier over a text-based follow-up like a direct message, WhatsApp or email.

Ok go ahead… plot out which Value Add piece you're going to include at each of your follow-ups. Don't worry, you can alter this later. In fact, I'd encourage it! If you find that most chilly leads reply to a particular piece – budge it up the follow-up process a little. Test and refine, and adapt where you need to.

Key takeaways

- Gather folders of 'Value Add' pieces, that your ideal client will like (not that you decide you want to send – it's not about you!)
- Mix up the media, include video, pdfs, books, memes, coupon codes etc.
- Plot the Value Add column.

Chapter 13
Calls to Action

Section 13.1: Why Add a CTA?

The most fabulous sales message in the world doesn't matter if it doesn't drive people to take action and encourage them to purchase. It may not be an out-and-out pitch of "buy buy buy" but leading the prospective client to engage in some way must encourage them towards purchase. And if they have kept you hanging despite several follow-up attempts, you just want them to re-engage! "Hello… is anybody there…?"So how do we encourage them to do something to both engage and signal to us that they're still in the game? Well, that'll be the Call to Action (CTA). These little nuggets of oomph hold the key to propelling your sales process forward while establishing you as a reliable and helpful ally to your leads.

From sparking curiosity to driving action, CTAs are the secret sprinkles that help the lead move forwards, and keep you motivated as you see them engaging. Don't worry about the CTA seeming sleazy; it really doesn't have to be "buy now" or "call me"; you can switch them up. In fact, I'd recommend it! Don't keep asking them to do the same thing if it's not working. As always, go back to your ideal client avatar work and think about the CTAs you could use for them. It might be that scheduling a call or meeting with you would be a step too far for a shy lead. The same goes for a busy one. But downloading an exciting quick guide to something might be OK. Or a quick reply to a simple question is low-commitment enough for them to take the step. Think carefully about the type of CTA and how often you can combine it with your Value Add piece.

The point is, you've had a great conversation with a lead, or had a promising enquiry land in your inbox, you've perhaps shared valuable insights, and maybe feel you've already built a genuine connection. You've shared time together, man! But then, *crickets* – an awkward silence, or a glaring absence of an email reply. The call you were sure would come into your phone doesn't materialise.

Now is not the time to rock in the corner eating ice cream. As I said, nice as that would be it's not going to pay the bills and get you to target.

Now is not the time to give up, either. We already know that some buyers take more following up than others. They may just not be ready right now. In fact 50% of them aren't ready to buy yet:

"50% of leads are qualified but not yet ready to buy."

(Source: Gleanster Research)

So – it's up to you to show the way forward, and be there for when they ARE ready.

Section 13.2
Types of CTA

Without a roadmap provided by a powerful CTA, your leads may wander aimlessly, unsure of their next move. Time ticks away, and you find yourself waiting, waiting, and waiting some more. In this waiting game, control slips through your fingers, and the momentum you worked so hard to build fizzles away. The opportunity for a seamless and confident follow-up slips by, leaving you feeling unsure of how to rekindle the conversation.

Not only that, but you may also find yourself scrambling to reconnect, trying to revive a conversation that has lost its spark. The awkwardness that ensues can be palpable – the once vibrant connection is now tainted by the silence and indecision. You wonder how you let this happen and kick yourself for not having had a simple CTA in place. Let's make no bones about it; it's your fault. Sorry, my friend. It's your job to nurture the leads, not theirs to run after you begging to buy. So – have a plan. Oh, yes, that's why we are here! We need to build it!

Let's banish awkward silences and regain control of the follow-up process once and for all! Because if we don't, your competitor may step in, take control of their buying journey and guide them away from you. We're not having that!

Time to give you some examples.

As I said, we can link the CTA to your Value Add in a very natural way. Here are some suggestions to get you started.

- Your Value Add is an article link, so your CTA could be to ask their thoughts on it or if they found the same thing (or whatever question fits), to encourage them simply to reply with a thought/comment.

- Your Value Add is a case study of how you gave a quick win to a past client and your CTA is a "book a call" link to your calendar, maybe for a 15-minute call so they don't see hours of their day being swallowed up.
- Your Value Add is an invitation to an event of some description – the CTA could be a "sign up" button or a "reply to me with 'yes' and I'll send over your ticket."
- Your Value Add is a fun meme or gif sent over WhatsApp – your CTA could be "send me an emoji of how your day is going."

Here is a list of Calls To Action – it is not exhaustive, so add your own!

- book a call
- fill in this form
- attend a webinar
- come to our Live
- reply to my email/WhatsApp
- click this link
- download this thing
- take this quiz
- grab this discount code
- request a demo/free trial
- have a video/FaceTime tour
- get extra free/free thing with this code
- watch this video
- contact this past client for a reference (you'll need their permission of course)
- ask a very simple question

Section 13.3
Plotting the CTA

Now, grab your trusty Framework and think about each follow-up. We know the "when". We know the "how". And we have the Value Add for each one. Now, which CTA would your ideal client be most likely to take in each of these? Add it in.

Complete the Framework outline with your CTAs and make sure they are easy peasy. If you want anyone to do anything – making it easy is the first step to getting it done.

Try to ensure that any forms your leads will have to complete are as simple as possible. Having said that, do include the phone or WhatsApp number, as you'll need this for follow-up calls.

Make sure the offer – download, video or whatever your value add is – is easy to consume, download or access and gives them a taster of how fantastic it would be to work with you.Right, all done? Then it's time to move on to implementing the Framework!

Key takeaways

- Decide on your calls to action options
- Range them from low to higher commitment
- Plot them in the Framework

Part IV
Getting It Done

By this point you should have your Follow-Up Framework drawn up, an example is opposite. You have each column figured out, so for every row, or every Follow-up, you know exactly when you're doing what, how, and what value you're adding. Nice job!

Now it's time to put it into action. I'm going to ask you to start as quickly as possible, as every lead you leave to go cold is a lead that will need warming up again, so everything you do now is saving you time later.

Follow up number	When?	How?	Value Add?	Call to Action?
Follow-up 1 Enquiry IN/ Outbound connection	Within 5 minutes if possible	The same way they enquired/ As agreed (usually email)	Calendly link for chat	(calendly link) Book a chat
Follow-up 2	+1 day	Call (or voicemail and email)	Helpful pdf download	Download pdf
Follow-up 3	+2 days	Call (or voicemail and email)	Further info or case study	Book a chat
Follow-up 4	+2 days	Whatsapp (or text)	Video/imgaes of destinations	Book a chat
Follow-up 5	+3 days	Call (or voicemail and email)	Pdf guide to xxx	Download
Follow-up 6	+3 days	Video message (whatsapp/email)	(video message)	Book a chat
Follow-up 7	+2 days	Call (or voicemail and email)	A few FAQs answered	Book a chat
Follow-up 8	+7 days	Social media DM	Some pics of past students or testimonials	Reply with questions

Chapter 14
Stop Faffing

One client of mine had her plan mapped out. It was good to go: ready to start using. But she wanted to keep it on her desk, so she didn't forget the steps. Fair enough, I thought. When I got back in touch with her a week later and asked how it was going she was delighted to tell me she had made progress! Brilliant! However, she hadn't actually started implementing it yet. She had made it into a beautiful piece of desk candy. It had colour-coded Value Add pieces, it was laminated and propped up on its own little stand. Which is all fabulous… but basically as useful as a chocolate teapot.

Something was stopping her from moving forward. We needed to do some digging around to find out what it was.

It turned out, her barrier was the fear of failure. She had some "what ifs" floating around that weren't being addressed.

What if…

I do all these follow-ups and still don't make a sale?

I do it wrong and annoy the leads?

The mindset monkeys had come out to play again. And we all have them. I've been selling for three decades and still have the odd wobble. When we are talking about leads it is a quality AND a quantity game. In my call with this client she had tried to make ten calls on her first follow-up. Of those ten calls, five were voicemails (she hadn't actually left a voicemail – she wasn't sure what to say so we have since practised that. After all, for the sake of an extra two or three seconds you may as well leave a nice impression). And of those ten calls, four had been connected but three of those weren't with the decision maker on her list. Only on one of the calls had she got through to the decision maker.

It hadn't started well, then. Even with the call that reached the decision maker, they had been in the middle of a meeting and brusquely asked her to call back.

She asked me what she was doing wrong. There were some tweaks we could make to her voicemails. There were some techniques to use on the gatekeepers to fix appointments when the decision makers were back.

But the biggest tweak was to do more outreach. Ten simply isn't enough. Ten had taken her 15 minutes. I had to deliver a little tough love. Fifteen minutes, once, isn't enough.

Follow-up is a daily sales task – like prospecting. It should be in your calendar. It should be non-negotiable if you want to save money and convert more leads into sales.But I understand that it can be disheartening if you have rolled up your sleeves, built yourself up to make some follow-up calls and then you don't strike gold straight away. Remember, this is a long game. Sales follow-up is like regularly going to the gym; it's not about setting a world record on your first visit; it's about consistent effort over time. Each day you show up and do the work, you're not only improving individual "muscles" but also building your overall "fitness" (or sales prowess). While any single workout (or follow-up) might not seem transformational, the cumulative effect can be dramatic. In both sales and fitness, the numbers game is won through persistence, routine, and a commitment to making incremental gains every single day.

The Framework is there for a reason. It will help you more sales. You didn't spend this time making the Framework to not bother using it. You know the statistics, you know it's the right process. But still the monkeys are having a fabulous time dancing around and stomping on your confidence.

You have become too attached to the outcome. Each follow-up has appeared to be a make-or-break situation. After 10 outreaches, if nobody has bitten your arm off, you're going to give up.
It's a mindset trap that many salespeople find themselves falling into. When you're overly attached to a specific outcome, like making an immediate sale or securing a big deal, it can create a cloud of pressure and anxiety that hinders your follow-up efforts.Picture this scenario: you've had a great conversation with a potential lead, and you are practically chalking up the sale. You're already envisioning the commission you'll earn and the boost you'll feel. But then, as you follow-up with the lead, you notice that they're not responding as quickly as you'd hoped. Doubt begins to creep in, and you start questioning your abilities. You worry that your service or product isn't up to scratch after all. You start to think that your competitors are winning and you're left without the sale. Does this sound familiar? I have been there, my friend. I still go there, too! This doesn't go away, though it does soften, I promise. The difference is that now you have a plan. You have thoughtfully considered your Follow-Up Framework. It's time to start to trust the process.

So what can we actually DOOOO? Well – I'm not about to abandon you to fluffiness now – let's look at practical ways to move on and get started.

Firstly, remember it's not about YOU. It's about the lead. That person or company needs you in their life! You just need to lead the way through the process to check they are a fit, and help them with all the information they need. Instead of fixating solely on the end result, let's flip the script and focus on what you can do to detach from the outcome while still keeping your eyes on the prize.

Secondly, remember that "no" is part of the process. A "no" means you gave it a shot and they just weren't ready to buy yet. That's OK. Keep to the Framework and follow-up; maybe they are not ready now, but they might be later. Others will say "yes" sooner, too.

As the oft-quoted Wayne Gredzy said: "You miss 100% of the shots you don't take." If you want to miss ALL possible sales, don't do the follow-up. Chuck the Framework away. Moreover, were you to only want to follow the Framework if you're guaranteed a 100% conversion rate – I can tell you now that won't happen. Well, it is highly unlikely but I guess it's possible, in which case, let's do lunch – you're paying.

So if that procrastination has crept in, here are some tips.

1) Embrace the Process: instead of obsessing over the final "yes" or "no," embrace the journey of building connections and nurturing relationships. Each follow-up is a chance to learn more about your leads, understand their needs, and add value to their lives. Not to mention the fact you can glean future sales points from these conversations. Enjoy the process! Enjoy the people!

2) Celebrate the Small Wins: don't overlook the little victories along the way. Did you have an engaging conversation with

a lead? Celebrate! Did they show genuine interest in your offerings? Applaud yourself! By acknowledging these mini milestones, you'll boost your confidence and motivation to keep going.

3) Reframe Rejection: repeat after me: "Rejection is not a reflection of my worth!" Sometimes leads say "no" because it's not the right time or fit for them. Instead of taking it personally, see it as an opportunity to fine-tune your approach and learn from the experience.

4) Add Value, not Pressure: focus on being a helpful resource rather than a pushy salesperson. Your genuine care and desire to solve your leads' problems and make their lives better will shine through and build trust. And trust is the magic ingredient to unlocking more opportunities.

5) Set Realistic Goals: yes, we all dream big, and that's fantastic! But set realistic expectations for each follow-up. Sometimes a lead needs time to consider their options (remember that 40% aren't ready to buy yet), so give them space while staying on their radar with gentle nudges.

6) Practice Mindfulness: stay present in each follow-up interaction. Be fully engaged, listen actively, and respond thoughtfully. This mindfulness will keep you grounded and prevent your mind from wandering into the dangerous territory of "what-ifs". You probably don't like it if you think someone has zoned out in a conversation with you – so don't do it to your leads either.

7) Focus on Growth: Every "no" is a stepping stone to a "yes." Accept that rejection is going to happen. In fact, embrace rejection as a chance to grow and improve your skills. Ask for

feedback, analyse what worked, and keep refining your follow-up strategy.

Trust in your abilities, stay authentic, and be genuinely interested in your leads' needs. With each follow-up, you'll gain valuable insights and build lasting connections. And remember, the right opportunities will flow your way when you let go of the outcome and focus on adding value.

- Key takeaways Ensure you know what your ideal clients look like.
- Target them with laser focus in your marketing.
- When leads come into your world, qualify them early on.
- Ensure you know exactly what your qualifying criteria are.
- Ensure you know what dis-qualifies a lead also.
- Decide how you will deal with dis-qualified leads.

FREE EXTRA RESOURCES:

If you are flagging, and can't get your head into the right space, watch this quick video I have made for just such an occasion! https://www.nofluff.biz/spend-less-sell-more

Chapter 15
Form Your Follow-Up Habit

The Follow-Up Framework is really there to help you follow up quiet leads – particularly when you don't really feel like it! If they reply to one of your follow-ups, then you do what you would clearly do as a polite human; reply to their questions, offer some added value and – yes – set the next step with them. And celebrate – the fact you have reheated the lead!

If they go quiet on you again – go back to the Follow-Up Framework and carry on.

Before you start

Follow-up, like prospecting, is a daily task in sales. It is going to move the needle on your sales speedometer. As we are humans and we like to get feedback, and as you don't always get that while making calls and emails in your follow-up, you may go off the boil. But please think of your follow-up tasks as part of your daily habits. Like brushing your teeth, and going for a walk or run (or whatever it is you do), it needs to be done, so let's get it done. You have, by now, read the statistics and reasoning behind a robust Follow-Up Framework, so you know it is important. Now it's just establishing the habit!

We are going to sidestep here into the principles of habit formation, drawing inspiration from the insights of James Clear's book, *Atomic Habits*. If you haven't read it, do – it's fascinating and practical. I read it several years ago and have used some of the theories and practices in my own work and with clients. Here are the ones I found most useful when it comes to establishing a healthy Follow-Up habit.

1) The Power of Tiny Steps:

   James Clear reminds us that even the tiniest changes can lead to remarkable results. Let's begin with small, manageable steps, like committing to just one 15-minute session of follow-up each day. Like building blocks, these daily efforts will eventually construct a solid foundation for lasting success. Set a date in the diary to review how it went. Then build it into a half-hour session every day. Again, diarise to check progress, and then move to including two half-hour sessions every day.

2) Creating Reliable Cues and Routines:

   Every successful habit requires a reliable cue and a consistent routine. This idea was a game-changer for me. Establish a specific time or trigger for your daily follow-up session. That could be commenting on leads' LinkedIn posts on the train ride; calling your follow-up list after your morning coffee; or sending your follow-up emails and texts straight after you get back from lunch. As the designated time approaches – and I'd recommend setting an alarm and blocking it in your calendar – immerse yourself in your follow-up routine, fully focused on connecting with your leads – don't get distracted by other shiny objects!

3) Temptation-Bundling for Motivation:

   Combine an enjoyable activity with your follow-up routine to create a good experience. You might want to sip a favourite drink or have some background music on while engaging in your follow-up tasks. I am a sucker for a fizzy sugar-free drink, so my afternoon follow-up is around 3pm when I go grab a bottle of something orange or brown from the fridge and settle in to do my follow-up. I tell myself I am not allowed the drink if I don't do my follow-up. This motivational trick will make follow-up an eagerly anticipated part of your daily routine.

4) Embracing Positive Reinforcement:

   Celebrate each completed follow-up session with a small reward. Positive reinforcement strengthens your habit, reinforcing the connection between the task and the feeling of accomplishment. Personally, I love ticking tasks off a list, so I do that in my calendar or planner. I feel like I am "bossing" the day!

5) The Magic of Tracking Progress:

   Track your follow-up success with diligence. Regularly record your follow-up interactions in a spreadsheet or CRM. Witnessing your progress will fuel your motivation and keep you enchanted with the process. If you are doing this manually, just keep a daily tally of how many follow-ups you did (maybe by stage if you're good with spreadsheets), how many replied, how many you disqualified, and how many progressed. Don't focus on the daily results as there is always a day where you don't get through to anyone, but review it weekly, and monthly.

6) Do it together!

    Join forces with your team, or if you're working at home, try some virtual co-working. Accountability is a powerful driver, if you know someone else is turning up to do this follow-up, you're not likely to let them down. Make it a team effort, and gamify it! Moreover, every so often, discuss what worked, what didn't and make notes for when you tweak your Follow-Up Framework. For example, one colleague may always get engagement after sending a particular email with a particular piece of Value – emulate it! And move that Follow-up further towards the beginning of the Framework.

7) Embracing Patience and Perseverance:

    Mastering the daily follow-up habit requires patience and perseverance. The results won't show immediately (they might, though!). Understand that habit formation is an ongoing process. You wouldn't expect to go to the gym twice and come out with a six-pack (hey, maybe you had one going into the gym in the first place); it takes consistency.

Cultivate a positive mindset, staying committed to your daily ritual.

Again, go grab James Clear's book if you can! But complete your Follow-Up Framework first!

While every lead is different, it can help to dedicate time blocks throughout your day to your follow-up. I am a big fan of time blocking and use it through much of my sales training. Many of my clients now have calendars with times blocked off for "prospecting calls", "follow-up", "upselling", "customer check in", as well as "take a break" and "professional development". Unless you commit to it, it may get shuffled out of the way.

So, head into your calendar now, and set a repeated slot, every working day, for your follow-up, starting with half an hour. If you are lucky enough to have a support team and your entire day is lead outreach, then it'll be more. Try to link them to another habit, as James Clear advises. This could be after a regular meeting, with your morning coffee, or after lunch. This will make it easier to establish your newfound habit and lead to you uncovering hidden gems in that pipeline.

Key Takeaways:

- Set regular times in your diary for sales actions
- Link sales actions to other habits
- Celebrate doing the hard work!

FREE EXTRA RESOURCES:

Time can seem like our enemy. I am not an expert time management trainer, but have tried, tested, and developed techniques over the years. I had to; at one point I was a single parent, with a single income, starting No Fluff, my new business; maintaining my existing job, moving house, and homeschooling my daughter. I had to learn FAST how to manage my time and prioritise! If you want my top tips and the methods I use, you can grab a free download at the extra resources section
https://www.nofluff.biz/spend-less-sell-more

Chapter 16
Dusting off the Diamonds

By this point you should be on board with the need for Follow-up. And you have your Framework ready to rock. But you still feel you'll start this from now on, a new chapter, a new beginning! No lead will go untended!

I promise you, there is a treasure trove of leads you've interacted with in the past, now lying dormant somewhere in the vast expanse of your CRM or inbox. These leads hold potential for conversions, growth, and for boosting your sales figures. But there they sit, waiting for the right nudge, the right spark, to reignite their interest. You left them.

Just because these leads have been silent doesn't mean they're disinterested. They might have been sidetracked, their attention captured by the whirlwind of life. Your mission? To remind them of your value proposition, reignite their curiosity, and steer them back into your sales journey.

So, gather your enthusiasm, realise that at this point you have absolutely nothing to lose, and let's breathe new life into these forgotten leads. You will rebel against this. You will feel uncomfortable. But I know this works.

In a free sales challenge I ran just after a Covid lockdown had lifted, one of the tasks was to contact leads that had gone very cold and you'd given up on. This was where I lost a few people! They weren't prepared to go out of their comfort zone. They forgot that it isn't about their own feelings, but those of the potential clients. But, wow, for those who did it, they came back with the treasure. They were able to set up meetings to rekindle the interest. One education agent warmed up a "group leader" prospect and sold a group of 30 places on a summer program within one phone call. And one language school BDM sold £170,000 worth of placements from leads "…that were just sitting there! That I'd completely given up on!". If that is what happens in just one session of reaching out to your cold, given-up-on leads, just think what you have in there.

It's just a question of getting past that first squirm!

Are you in? Yes! Let's do it! As you set out on the path of rekindling old leads, it's important to understand why they went dormant in the first place. Dormancy doesn't necessarily equate to disinterest; it often arises due to various external factors that divert attention elsewhere. Perhaps life got busier, priorities shifted, or circumstances changed. They may even have purchased from a competitor, but not all purchases last a lifetime – they may be up for renewal, or they may not have got the service they would like.

The point is – you don't know, unless you try.

And the other point is – if they bought from a competitor, they SPEND on your solution. They are a stronger lead. So please don't be put off!

Remember, these leads were once intrigued by your offering, which means the potential for rekindling that spark is very much alive. So, as you move forward, let's explore the factors that lead to dormancy and how you can address them strategically. It's all part of the grand plan to turn silent prospects into enthusiastic buyers.

Now that you've laid the groundwork by understanding why leads go dormant, it's time to craft messages that will rekindle their interest. Your re-engagement messages should resonate with the recipients, reminding them of the value you offer and reigniting their curiosity about your product or service.

The key here is personalisation. Generic messages won't cut it when re-engaging dormant leads. Refer back to your previous interactions, highlight any shared experiences, and make them feel like you remember them. Share relevant updates, new offerings, or insights that align with their interests.

Consider using storytelling to evoke emotions and reconnect on a human level. Show empathy, address any potential concerns they might have had, and position yourself as a helpful resource rather than a pushy salesperson. By focusing on value and personalisation, you increase the chances of grabbing their attention and prompting a response.

And this is why I like the good old phone call. It is the epitome of personalisation. They may well be surprised to hear from you, and in some cases an SMS may be good to start with, but the sole aim of this first outreach is to pique their interest.CASE STUDY: The Hidden Treasure

A wonderful education counsellor that I have worked with is a driven, ambitious and caring woman. She knows her worth, she's great at what she does, and is busy. However, this can mean that, if a potential client doesn't engage with her and her services pretty swiftly, she assumes they don't see her value and she moves on. After all, there are plenty of fish in the sea.

However, when I was in her office one day I encouraged her to go through old leads on her CRM. Dig right back through those that didn't progress, and call them.

This lady trusts me; we have worked together for a while and she knows that when I guide her, it works. So although she was cringing, she called them.

In the half an hour or so we did this, she made five calls to very old, and very cold, leads.She didn't really want to. But she did it, and for her trust in me, I am grateful.

Let me give you a breakdown of how it went.

Call #1: the lead got cross and said to not call again.

Call #2: the lead was pleased to hear from her and chatted about their plans, and arranged another consultation.

Call #3: the lead was on holiday but was happy to hear from her, remembered her and asked to be called back after her holiday to talk further.

Call #4: the lead was again happy to hear from her; they talked about the original enquiry and they had bought from someone else in the end, but were considering buying again so they arranged another call after information was sent.

Call #5: the lead remembered her, and thanked her for the call but said they weren't looking for this service at the moment, but would be happy to attend the upcoming webinar and to send the sign-up details.

Admittedly, the first call was a bit of a bad moment! I think if I hadn't been there to encourage her she would have given up there. But having cross people on the phone is pretty rare, especially if they have already engaged with you in some way. Four out of five of these calls were very positive, only one was negative. In my experience, fewer than one in 30 are negative, so it was a bit of bad luck on this occasion it was the first call.For the other calls, two booked further consultations – so they were successfully re-ignited. One wanted to be called back – fair enough. But also re-ignited. And one dis-qualified himself by saying they weren't looking for this service right now, but then agreed to attend an event, so they defrosted a little.

Not bad for ½ hour.

And the beauty of this is that if she spends half an hour per day, only half an hour, doing this, and gets a similar success rate of gaining two consultations per day, that is golden. Once this lady has a consultation, her conversion rate is around 60%. So for each week of spending half an hour per day on chilly leads she can gain ten consultations, and after they have been through her follow-up framework and consultancy process, that will convert to an average of six new sales per week.And let's be clear. This is ten consultations from leads she had given up on. She had already spent the marketing cash on attracting those leads to enquire. She had already spent time on a few follow-up calls, and sometimes with a consultation, but they hadn't bought. So by re-approaching them she is uncovering hidden gems of clients. With zero extra spend, and within two and a half hours of re-engagement work per week.

Worth the squirm?

Start planning it into your diary.

Chapter 17
Automation

Now, this is a big subject, and I will only touch on it in this book. I hesitated before writing this section because I have seen, first-hand that setting up all the fancy automations can lead to a delay on actually getting the work done. When I checked in with a client I worked with recently on their Follow-Up Framework, they hadn't implemented it at all after two weeks. When I asked why – he said he was waiting for "marketing" to set up all the automations with the emails to head out. Even if he had to wait for that (which he didn't, as he could have done it manually while he was waiting), he could still call, WhatsApp and DM. He was completely procrastifaffing as it was much easier to pass the buck to marketing and blame them. No, the buck stops with whoever needs to make the sale. If your job is to bring in the deals, you can start the Follow-Up Framework straight away. You could even be refining those templates and the touchpoints before it goes into an automation. Please don't let setting up your automations slow you down. You are losing sales as you wait, thus leaving money on the table. It is avoidance. (OK, tough love part now over.)

From scheduling reminders to automatically diarising the next follow-up steps, automation within your Customer Relationship Management (CRM) system can, however, transform your daily routine. The aim is to make it easier for you to implement your Follow-Up Framework.

Now, if you can, integrate your Follow-Up Framework into your CRM. With a few clicks, your CRM can be programmed to generate reminders for follow-up calls, meetings, or emails. No more sifting through scattered notes or relying on memory – the system ensures that you never miss an important interaction. As you input the details of each follow-up, the technology takes over, freeing you to concentrate on crafting personalised messages and strengthening client relationships.

The world of sales CRMs is a big one, so again, I won't go into it here, but examples you may have heard of are Salesforce, HubSpot, Pipedrive and Zoho, and there are a gazillion bespoke options out there too. They do not have to be big expensive investments if you are a small business and worried about cost; there is, for example, a free sales CRM from HubSpot and their starter package is around £30 a month. I would highly recommend a CRM, if you don't already have one, as, if you are using Excel or a similar spreadsheet it can become unwieldy, and looking up your follow-up dates becomes an eye-straining task. And if we don't find something easy, we are much more likely to procrastinate around it. Get your Follow-Up Framework timings onto a nice CRM calendar which will also pop up with a suggestion for the next task so you don't forget to apply your Follow-Up Framework.

If you don't have a sales CRM at the moment, don't let that stop you getting going with your Follow-Up Framework. Pop "Research sales CRMs" into your diary sometime and go ahead and use a spreadsheet and a calendar for the moment. Just be mindful to always set that next step. Simply note under the client what follow-up you just did, what happened, and diarise the next one in your Framework in your calendar. What you don't want to do is forget that next step or you'll start leaking those leads again.

While we are touching on the subject of automation, it can be a massive time-saver. Pinging off preset emails or messages can save time, qualify prospects and lead to sales. Personally, I believe this is better for audience warm up and lead generation than closing of higher ticket, nuanced or more personalised sales, but it can work for "off the shelf" offers too.

Automated sequences can certainly mirror the cadence we've been perfecting in our Follow-Up Framework. However, instead of individually composing each call with a personal touch or tailoring every follow-up email with customised finesse, automation takes the lead, orchestrating the performance seamlessly.

But – again sorry (not sorry) for the tough love – don't let the allure of automation lull you into complacency – automation isn't a substitute for genuine human connection. While it can boost efficiency, relying exclusively on automated responses could inadvertently dilute the authentic touch that human interaction brings. Today's leads, particularly the tech-savvy millennials and Gen Z, have a keen sense for standardised interactions. They yearn for authenticity, an individualised connection that algorithms cannot replicate. If you've ever used a chatbot that you spent twenty minutes with that before it said it can't help and you need to contact customer services, you will understand that automation can do more harm than good.

In a world where authenticity reigns supreme, it's a delicate balance between automation and personal touch. Use automation as your support system, streamlining tasks and extending your reach. However, let your unique sales skills shine, building relationships that go beyond digital barriers. Remember, your leads are more than just entries in a database; they're individuals seeking genuine connections.

Moreover, the more direct and varied your communication with potential customers, the more adept you become at predicting objections, refining your offers, and nurturing rapport. While text-based interactions play a role, it's the fabulous mash-up of voice, in-person meetings, and digital exchanges that truly creates a powerful combination.

That said, we can set ourselves up to save some time, with or without automation.

Key Takeaways:

- Set up automations to help you complete your sales tasks.
- Don't rely on automation if you want to convert individual buyers better.

Chapter 18
Templates and Prompts

Who likes life to be a bit easier? Me me me! If I can save myself some time and yet still make my leads feel important, I am up for some templates, prompts, and strategic organisation. The easier I make it for myself, the more likely I am to do the task, in this case, the follow-up.Picture this: Follow up #3 is designated as an email. Here's your chance to craft a template, incorporating the Value Add you've planned and a compelling Call To Action. You've spent time on what to say, how to say it and kept your ideal client avatar in mind. Beautiful. Now, let's keep it tucked away as a draft, primed and ready for action. When the moment arrives, simply add a dash of personalised information to infuse that human touch. This could refer back to their initial inquiry or a prior conversation – an indicator that you've been paying attention. And if specific details are sparse, add your own personal touch so it doesn't sound like a robot wrote it. Let's face it, mentioning the local weather never goes out of style – I mean, I'm British, and it's practically a national pastime! Remember to make the messages resonate with your voice, catered to your ideal client avatar and tailored to your unique offer.

Now let's look at the calls in your Follow-Up Framework, like Follow-up #4. In your Framework you have some conversational prompts, the Value Add part and the Call To Action. This prevents those awkward fallbacks like "Did you get my email?" or the classic "I was just following up." Instead, weave in the Value Add – "I noticed your company's up for an award – congratulations!" Or recall a past discussion – "Remember when we talked about X? I came across this fantastic article on the topic." These prompts are your conversation starters, but remember, authenticity is always the key. If "Hi!" doesn't quite match your usual tone, then skip it. So, wield the power of personalisation, let your own voice shine through, and watch your follow-ups transform into meaningful conversations.

A step further:

Now, don't judge – I like to keep my follow-ups in nicely labelled template folders (you do you, I'll do me.). When I first started building my Framework I used pretty much the same follow-up templates and prompts for everyone. Now I have a selection of folders according to the type of ideal client avatar and also for different services.

For example, my follow-up with a lead that is interested in my high ticket "done for you" service (in which I set up their whole sales function including technology, templates, training etc) would have different pieces of value to someone keen on my lower ticket offer. Not always, but the further you go into this the more you can adjust and refined.

Here is an example of my filing:

Low ticket – ideal client avatar #1
FU1 – call prompt
FU2 – e template
FU3 – call prompt
FU4 – DM prompt
FU5 – text/WhatsApp template
FU6 – call prompt
FU7 – video message prompt
FU8 – e template
FU9 – call prompt

I have a file of Value Adds. So also, in case the lead has already been through my Framework before or I feel a different one would be more relevant, I slot one of these in instead.

Value Add
Social Proof (subfolders by type of client and by product)
External articles (subfolders by area of relevance)Case Studies (subfolders by type of client and product)
Fun (subfolders memes, gifs, stories, playlists)
Events (where to meet me, free webinars)

Chapter 19
Put it All into Practice

TEMPLATES FOR EMAILS:

1. "The Educational Article"

Subject: [their name], you might like this article on [relevant topic]

Hi [name],

How is life at [their company name] today?

[add in personalised reference].

I came across this article on [relevant topic] and thought it might be of interest to you. It offers some unique insights that could benefit [their business or specific interest].

[Link to the article]

Let me know what you think, perhaps over a virtual coffee

on Thursday if you have ten minutes? How does 2pm sound?

Regards, [Your Name]

2. "The Exclusive Offer"

Subject: I made you a Special Offer [name]

Hi [name],

I was so keen to work with you in our last discussion and I value your interest; to show my appreciation, I have secured an exclusive offer just for you. [Describe the offer in a sentence].

Could we have a quick chat so you can see if that would work for you? Maybe Wednesday? Here's my diary link to pick whenever suits you, it'll be fantastic to go over it and help you progress [(towards the outcome they originally wanted].

See you soon, [your name]

3. "The Testimonial"

Subject: See How [company/customer name] [got to a similar outcome]!

Hello [Name],

Our earlier conversation came to mind when I read this success story – [company/customer name] achieved [specific Relevant Result] with our help.

[Excerpt in text, link or attachment with the full testimonial]

I'm excited that we can get you there too. And beyond! Could we set a time to explore how this might apply to your situation?

Here is my WhatsApp if you want to just drop me a note with some times when you're free [enter number]

Speak soon, [your name]

4. "The Product/Service Update"

Subject: You're the first we're telling: New Updates to [product/service name]

Dear [name],

It's time to get excited! Since we last spoke, there have been some fantastic updates to our [product/service name]. I believe these changes can further benefit your [specific needs/goals].

Can we set up a call next week to go over how these enhancements will [enter outcome they wanted here eg. grow your business]?

I can't wait to hear your feedback, [your name]

5. "The Invitation to Event"

Subject: Exclusive Invitation: [event name]

Hi [Name],

You're on the VIP list! Given your interest in [specific topic/field], I'd like to personally invite you to [event name]. It's a unique opportunity to network and learn more about [event topic].

Will you be available? I'd love to catch up there. Here is the link to confirm you can attend, it only takes 30 seconds and then you're on the VIP list.

Looking forward to seeing you there,

Warmly, [your name]

6. "The Funny One"

Subject Just to make you smile today [name]

Hi [name]

I just wanted to share a quick chuckle with you.

(enter joke/meme/funny short story/gif)

A little smile to help your day along! Or was it a cringe?!

I hope we can chat soon, even if it's just a catch-up to see how you're going.

Smiles, [your name]

Phone Call Prompts to Get You Started

1) I was reviewing our last conversation and had a few ideas that could benefit your [specific challenge/need]. Is that the right challenge? Do you have a few minutes to discuss?
2) I wonder if you would help? Could you give me some feedback? We really value it from potential partners like you. Could you share any reservations or questions you might still have about [product/ service]? It'll help us serve you better and others, too.
3) I recently attended a webinar on [relevant topic] and gained some insights I thought could benefit you. Do you have a moment to chat about them?
4) I wanted to reintroduce our [product/service] as we've made some really exciting changes that I think you'd value. Can we discuss?
5) Just a quick call to remind you about our upcoming event, [event name]. Given your interest, I think you'd find it valuable. Will you be attending? I'd love to arrange a time to catch up there.

Of course, these sound a bit stilted here in the pages of this book. So feel free to adjust these templates and prompts according to your specific needs and target audience.

Navigating lead engagement is no small feat. But this is why we built your Follow-Up Framework. You have the Framework, and you have crafted the emails, texts and calls to fit.

The overarching goal? To maintain, or to reignite that initial spark of interest. Don't forget, they are not all ready to buy straight away, so this Framework is designed to catch all those leads that otherwise you would have let drift away.

Just in case you are flagging, I'd like to remind you of a few reasons why you need this One-Page Follow-Up Framework.

REMINDERS:

- **You want to get 80% of possible sales, not 10%**
- 10% of salespeople make more than three follow-ups, yet 80% of sales are made on the fifth to twelfth contact (Grant Cardone). You need to follow-up more.
- **You want more sales and lower costs.**
- Companies that excel at lead-nurturing generate 50% more sales-ready leads at 33% lower cost. (Forrester Research)
- **You want to be the one leads go to when they are ready to buy.**
- 50% of leads are qualified but not yet ready to buy. (Gleanster Research)
- **You want them to say yes.**
- 60% of customers say no four times before saying yes. (Invesp) You need to get through some no's first.
- **You want leads to make bigger purchases.**

Chapter 20
Reiterating the "Why bother?"

Nurtured leads make 47% larger purchases than non-nurtured leads.

(Source: The Annuitas Group)

First and foremost, even if they are ghosting you, you need to stay on their radar. In our digitised age, it's easy to become one of many fleeting memories in a crowded inbox. Regular, meaningful touchpoints keep you from becoming one email among many being bumped down their inbox. This is not just about being seen; I also want you to be remembered.

Secondly, we want to assert your expertise in the field. They need to know that you are the one they need to help reach their goals! YOU! They don't know it yet, that's all! This isn't about grandiose boasting but subtly showcasing the depth of your knowledge. Share updates, industry breakthroughs, or even intriguing tidbits that provide value. Tell them about events you're speaking at, accreditations you just achieved, high feedback scores you just had from a recent client. Make them realise that, by choosing you, they're aligning with a true industry guru. Make them want to be part of your circle.

However, knowledge alone isn't enough. It's vital to cultivate trust. This intangible, yet invaluable commodity is built through transparency, consistency, and genuine engagement. Each follow-up is an opportunity, a brick in the palace of trust you're building together. For large or personal ticket purchases, such as annual big bucks contracts, education for a child, personal development, trust is essential. Revisit your ideal client avatar and make a list of things they need to see and hear from you in order to help them build trust.

Also, it's important to offer insights that align with their goals. Tailored advice, resources, or tips can demonstrate that you're not just invested in a sale, but in their unique journey. Understand their pain points and aspirations, and let your follow-up content help them.

While knowledge, trust, and insights are foundational, sometimes all a lead needs is a gentle nudge. Prompt them to take even minor actions, maybe reading a blog post, checking out a new feature, or just replying to your email. Each tiny step is progress, steering them closer to decision-making. And the more baby steps they take, the better.

I'll add something here a little about gratitude. Always reinforce your appreciation for their potential business, and for each little step taken. I don't mean start tugging your forelock and being creepy, but genuine gratitude. Remember that they had a choice especially if competition is fierce in your sector. This not only nurtures a sense of mutual respect but also subtly reminds them of the value they are bringing to the table.

As you guide them, it can be valuable if you can create a sense of community or belonging to an exclusive "club". There's a unique allure in being part of something greater, a larger narrative. It can be reassuring if they know others that they respect have already joined this club. If they feel they're joining a community or a movement, the decision becomes emotionally charged, adding another layer of engagement. Often, where one goes, others will follow.

Occasionally, if it's possible, infuse your follow-ups with exclusivity or limited-time offers. They do not have to be discounts; they can be added extras. I'm aware that discounts in some markets are the way to go, but adding value rather than reducing price is a more robust plan and much easier on the bottom line. However, time-limited offers can work really well. The ticking clock or the allure of something exclusive can be the catalyst propelling them into action.

Showcase testimonials or success stories; these are likely to resonate more than a sales pitch. Let them see the satisfied smiles, the success narratives, and the data (if data-led outcomes are what they are looking for). This instils confidence and paints a picture of potential outcomes for them. It inspires them to take action if they can see themselves in your story's hero's shoes.

Having said all that, I would love you to remember one thing; as you deftly guide them through this journey, always remember the end goal: to subtly steer them towards making that purchase. Otherwise, it's just a nice chat. Remember to ask for the sale, or offer the chance to buy, and don't forget those Calls To Action.

In essence, modern lead engagement isn't just about persistence; it's about empathy and genuine connection. Through strategic follow-ups, you're not just selling a product; you're curating an experience.

Conclusion

We've journeyed together through the maze of sales, and you've discovered tools that will not only save you time but also supercharge your success. Remember those alluring distractions of shiny marketing temptations? You've gained the wisdom to spend less cash and effort on them by focusing on the true gems – those ideal clients who align perfectly with your offerings. By honing the power to qualify or disqualify early, you've gained a potent weapon that targets your efforts where they matter most.

And of course, you have your Follow-Up Framework – the heart and soul of your sales conversions. This isn't just a roadmap; it's your guiding star, helping you engage with leads and transform them first into buyers, and then to loyal customers. As you embark on this next phase, remember that the Follow-Up Framework isn't a rigid structure; it's a living, breathing tool designed to adapt to your needs. You'll get started, test it, see which follow-ups convert better, bump them up the Framework and then tweak it with confidence. The next aim is to guide your buyers towards a sale faster, freeing up your time to work on other leads. This framework isn't static – it's a dynamic ally that evolves alongside you. Ideally you'd employ it consistently, across the whole team, if you have one. That way you can keep an eye on your conversion rates, number of touchpoints needed and average spend.

Right then! Now it's time to embark on a new phase of your journey. Imagine the transformation of your sales figures as you engage your leads with confidence, leading them toward a resounding "yes." You are building a family of fans who don't feel "sold to" but feel heard, understood, valued and nurtured through their buying journey. This isn't just about closing deals; it's about crafting relationships that withstand time.

So, here's your call to action: seize the moment. Put those strategies into motion, and let your Follow-Up Framework guide you through the process that will rocket your sales with purpose and precision.

As you take the next steps, remember this isn't about reaching a destination – though the sale is the main aim, it's about the journey, a journey filled with triumphs, growth, and evolution for both you and your leads. Your Follow-Up Framework isn't just a tool; it's your key to unlocking a new era of sales success, as you learn how to use helpful persistence and learn from each objection given, each Value Add that hits the right note and each conversion that comes in after what used to be the normal second and final follow-up. You'll start to see how many more sales you are making on the third, fourth, fifth follow-up that you would otherwise have given up on long ago. You'll follow the process and you'll still be surprised when, at the eighth follow-up, that lead that who has said "no" a few times, or ghosted you for maybe six months, says yes.

So, are you ready? I'm sure you are – the Follow-Up Framework is all done, don't delay it with excuses – you can start putting it into action today. It's time to step forward with confidence, knowing that you have the tools, the knowledge, and the power to convert more leads into sales, and more sales into lifelong customers. Go forth and follow up, these people need your fabulousness!

Acknowledgments

I would like to thank my family for putting up with months' of my early mornings writing this book; and my network for their encouragement along the way.

About the Author

Nicola Lutz is a sales coach and trainer, working predominantly in the international education sector. She has been selling and leading sales teams for 28 years since she graduated from Coventry University with an honours degree in French and Spanish. She is a Founding Fellow of the Institute of Sales Professionals, a keynote speaker and winner of several sector awards. She started her company, No Fluff, to help small and medium-sized businesses increase their sales, in a holistic way, without compromising on integrity. No ringing of bells, and no snake oil tactics.

She lives by the sea in Kent, and adores travel and learning about other cultures, but not before a big cup of coffee.

Endnotes

6:1 https://www.dataaxlegenie.com/blog/lead-nurturing-statistics/

6:2 https://ircsalessolutions.com/insights/sales-follow-up-statistics/

11:1 https://answernet.com/blog-generations-styles-communication/

11:2 https://www.smallbizgenius.net/by-the-numbers/cold-calling-statistics/

11:13 https://dma.org.uk/uploads/misc/5a1583ff3301a-consumer-email-tracking-report-2017-(2)_5a1583ff32f65.pdf

11:14 https://www.salesforce.com/blog/2017/08/personalize-every-email.html

11:15 https://www.superoffice.com/blog/email-open-rates

11:6 https://www.rainsalestraining.com/blog/6-common-linkedin-selling-mistakes-and-how-to-avoid-them

11:7 https://ircsalessolutions.com/insights/sales-follow-up-statistics/

11:8 https://www.salesloft.com/resources/blog/video-sales-emails-increases-reply-rate/

11:9 https://www.nielsen.com/insights/2012/consumer-trust-in-online-social-and-mobile-advertising-grows/

Printed in Great Britain
by Amazon

33326471R00106